THE
COUNT OF
MONTE CRISTO

This is a work of fiction. All of the characters, events, and organizations portrayed in this work are either products of the author's imagination or used fictitiously.

The Count Of Monte Cristo
Copyright © 2011 by Christopher M. Walsh

Based on the novel by Alexandre Dumas published in 1844.

Front cover photo by Suzanne Plunkett, featuring Christopher Hainsworth. Top back cover photo by Brandon Wardell, bottom left photo by Paul Metreyeon, bottom right photo by Suzanne Plunkett.

All rights reserved. No part of this book may be reproduced in any form by any electronic or mechanical means including photocopying, recording, or information storage and retrieval without permission in writing from the author.

ISBN-13: 978-0692356807
ISBN-10: 0692356800

For information about production rights, e-mail:
walsh.christopher@gmail.com

The Count of Monte Cristo

A PLAY BY
CHRISTOPHER M. WALSH

ADAPTED FROM THE NOVEL BY
ALEXANDRE DUMAS

The Count Of Monte Cristo received its world premiere at Lifeline Theatre in Chicago, IL, on September 14, 2011. It was directed by Paul S. Holmquist; original music and sound design was by Christopher Kriz; costume design was by Aly Renee Amidei; violence design was by Richard Gilbert and David Gregory; properties design was by Joe Schermoly; lighting design was by Brandon Wardell; scenic and properties design was by Joe Schermoly; and the production stage manager was Katie Adams. The cast was as follows:

Albert – Chris Daley
Benedetto/Franz – Jesse Manson
Caderhousse/Abbe Faria/Chairman – Don Bender
Danglars/Jailer 1 – John Ferrick
Fernand/Luigi Vampa/Jailer 2 – James Anthony Zoccoli
Edmond – Chris Hainsworth
Eugenie – Cathlyn Melvin
Haydee – Susaan Jamshidi
Hermine – Dana Black
Mercedes – Jenifer Tyler
Villefort – Robert Kauzlaric

Understudies – Scott T. Barsotti, Rachel Renee, Mandy Walsh

The following credit must appear in all programs/playbills handed to audience members at performances of The Count Of Monte Cristo:

The Count Of Monte Cristo was originally produced by Lifeline Theatre, Chicago, Illinois, and premiered there in 2011.

Cast of Characters

ALBERT - A young nobleman from Paris
BENEDETTO - A scam artist, thief, and murderer
CADERHOUSSE - A petty criminal
DANGLARS - A rich, corrupt baron and banker
FARIA - An intellectual priest, imprisoned for heretical ideas
FERNAND - A respected general
FRANZ - A young nobleman from Paris
EDMOND - A wealthy and mysterious nobleman
EUGENIE - A young noblewoman and artist
HAYDEE - A slave; once a Greek princess
HERMINE - A baroness
LUIGI VAMPA - An Italian bandit
MERCEDES - A countess
VILLEFORT - A powerful magistrate
CHAIRMAN
JAILERS 1 & 2
OTHERS - Servants, revelers, bandits, gendarmes, Peers, etc.

Setting

Multiple locations in and around Paris, Rome, and Marseilles, circa 1835; the dungeons of the Chateau d'If circa 1810-1825.

ACT I

Scene One

(Lights up. Moonlight wavers on the sea floor. The calm hum of the current is punctuated by the faint sound of waves crashing against rocks, high above. The waves increase in intensity as voices are heard, muffled, under water. The voices overlap, coming from everywhere, gradually become clearer)

MERCEDES
Edmond?

FARIA
Edmond, do you know what Providence is?

VILLEFORT
Who and what are you?

EDMOND
My name is Edmond Dantès.

VILLEFORT
Do you know what Providence is?

EDMOND
Mercedes?

MERCEDES
Edmond.

VILLEFORT
Edmond Dantès, you are under arrest.

FARIA
Fourteen years.

VILLEFORT
I am unable to restore you to liberty.

FARIA
Now there is a look I know well.

EDMOND
I was about to be married.

FARIA
It has instilled a new passion in your heart.

VILLEFORT
Do you know what Providence is?

FARIA
Vengeance.

MERCEDES
Edmond?

EDMOND
Her name is Mercedes.

FARIA
Do you know what Providence is?

VILLEFORT
Edmond Dantès, do you know what Providence is?

FARIA
Vengeance.

EDMOND
It is the will of God, sir.

FARIA
Providence.

VILLEFORT
You must avoid dwelling on what might be.

EDMOND
Her name is Mercedes. You must tell her.

VILLEFORT
You will surely go mad.

EDMOND
Mercedes. Mercedes!

(There is a great crash as a body wrapped in a shroud lands in the water)

FARIA
Do you know what Providence is?

(The body falls slowly at first, then with a sudden violent movement it writhes and twists, trying to free itself from the shroud. At last the shroud rips open and EDMOND emerges. He fights free from the shroud and swims away. Lights shift to a cave, revealing a heavy, ancient chest. An exhausted, bedraggled EDMOND enters. With great effort, he pries open the lid of the chest. He stares inside. Slowly, he reaches in and pulls out a handful of gems. There are so many they rain through his fingers. He picks one out and holds it up)

EDMOND
Danglars, my old friend and shipmate.

(EDMOND throws the jewel away. He holds up another one)

Fernand, dearest friend to my beloved.

(EDMOND throws the jewel away and takes another)

Monsieur Gerard de Villefort, honorable deputy prosecutor.

(He throws the jewel away and takes another)

Gaspard Caderousse, who saw it all and said nothing.

(He throws the jewel away and takes up another, this one bigger and brighter than all the rest)

Mercedes.

(EDMOND wraps his hands around the jewel and squeezes it tight)

Yes. I know what Providence is. It is the will of God.

(EDMOND slams the chest closed and exits)

Scene Two

(Lights shift to a street in Rome at the height of a festival. Revelers in masks run everywhere. ALBERT enters, also masked, and joins the party. He sees HAYDEE, also masked. She waves at him and then runs off. FRANZ enters. He and ALBERT remove their masks as they greet each other)

FRANZ
Albert!

ALBERT
Franz, my dear fellow! Did you see? I am convinced of the charms of Roman women.

FRANZ
How unfortunate that you were masked, Albert; here was an opportunity for you.

(HAYDEE, still masked, enters with several other revelers. She tosses a bouquet of violets to ALBERT before exiting)

FRANZ
Well, there is the beginning of an adventure.

ALBERT
Laugh if you will; I have decided to be in love.

(ALBERT exits, following HAYDEE. FRANZ exits in another direction. ALBERT re-enters, searching for HAYDEE. She enters behind ALBERT and surprises him. She starts to leave again, but ALBERT catches her hand and pulls her to him. Unseen by Albert, LUIGI VAMPA enters. As ALBERT reaches for HAYDEE's mask, LUIGI VAMPA aims a pistol at him)

LUIGI VAMPA
Sir.

(ALBERT turns to find himself surrounded by BANDITS. He turns back to HAYDEE, who smiles and waves, then exits)

LUIGI VAMPA
You see, sir, the streets are not safe at night.

ALBERT
So I've heard. And by whom do I have the honor of being kidnapped?

LUIGI VAMPA
Luigi Vampa, at your service. If you would be kind enough to follow me?

(LUIGI signals to one of the bandits, who approaches ALBERT. ALBERT surprises the bandit by attacking him. A brief melee breaks out, ending with ALBERT captured)

LUIGI VAMPA
This is not some romantic adventure, my friend. You

have heard what happens here in Italy? You will sign a letter. This letter demands a ransom, to be delivered by six o'clock tomorrow morning.

ALBERT
And if the money is not delivered?

LUIGI VAMPA
I think you know, my friend.

Scene Three

(Lights shift to the catacombs of an ancient Roman cemetery. ALBERT sleeps soundly. LUIGI VAMPA enters, followed by EDMOND, now dressed as the Count of Monte Cristo)

LUIGI VAMPA
Here he is, Excellency, as you requested. He signed the ransom note and promptly went to sleep. Not bad for a man who was told he'd be shot first thing in the morning. *(To ALBERT)* Awaken, sir!

ALBERT
Why? What time is it?

LUIGI VAMPA
Half past one, sir.

ALBERT
Has Franz come already?

LUIGI VAMPA
He has not.

ALBERT
Then what is it?

LUIGI VAMPA
A person to whom I can refuse nothing has come to demand you. May I present to you his excellency, the Count of Monte Cristo.

(LUIGI VAMPA bows to EDMOND and exits)

ALBERT
You really are most kind, but you must forgive me for asking who you are, and why you have chosen to bestow such generosity upon me?

EDMOND
I saw an opportunity. I have spent the last eight years traveling the Orient. I intend to travel to Paris soon. It is a city I have never seen. As a stranger there, I have only to ask you, my dear Viscount de Morcerf, whether you would undertake to open the doors of that fashionable world of which I know so little?

ALBERT
Oh, that I do, and with infinite pleasure. May I ask, how do you know my name, and how did you hear of my predicament?

EDMOND
By a complicated route, but suffice to say your friend Franz and I share the same banker in Rome.

ALBERT
And how did you secure my release without paying for it? Again, please don't think me ungrateful—

EDMOND
It was nothing. Your host and I are old acquaintances.

ALBERT
Friends with bankers and bandits! Are you truly a count?

EDMOND
I am, though newly made. I purchased my title in Tuscany.

ALBERT
Rich, too. And where is this Monte Cristo?

EDMOND
I shall gladly tell you all about it. However, we have overstayed the welcome of our gracious host, who would prefer we were not seen near his hideout by the light of day. If you will make your way toward the exit, I must have a brief word with Signore Vampa before we return to the city.

ALBERT
I'll wait for you on the road.

(ALBERT exits. HAYDEE enters, holding her mask. EDMOND takes her hand and kisses it with extreme formality. They exit separately)

Scene Four

(Flashback. Lights shift to Villefort's office. VILLEFORT and JAILER 1 enter. JAILER 1 hands VILLEFORT a letter, which VILLEFORT reads as he talks to the JAILER)

VILLEFORT
What is next?

JAILER 1
One Edmond Dantès, sir. The Bonapartist. *(VILLEFORT gives JAILER 1 a hard look)* Forgive me, sir. Accused Bonapartist.

VILLEFORT
The sailor. Details?

JAILER 1
We found this in his cabin on board the ship Pharaon.

(JAILER 1 hands a package of letters to VILLEFORT)

VILLEFORT
Is this all? Slim evidence. An anonymous note and a

packet of letters, unopened. Where did you find him?

JAILER 1
Ah... At a wedding, sir. His wedding.

VILLEFORT
I see. This fellow is having a singularly unfortunate day. Bring him in.

(JAILER 1 signals offstage. JAILER 2 enters, leading EDMOND. The JAILERS force EDMOND to sit. VILLEFORT signals for the JAILERS to exit)

VILLEFORT
I am the Deputy Prosecutor Gerard de Villefort. Who and what are you?

EDMOND
My name is Edmond Dantès. I am first mate aboard the merchant ship Pharaon.

VILLEFORT
Your age?

EDMOND
Nineteen.

VILLEFORT
This is all a misunderstanding, I am certain, and as soon as we clear it up you will be on your way. But we must observe the formalities. I want you to answer me not as a prisoner to a judge, but as one man to another. Do you understand?

EDMOND
I do.

VILLEFORT
What were you doing at the moment you were arrested?

EDMOND
I was about to be married, Monsieur. To a girl I have been attached to for three years. Her name is Mercedes.

(VILLEFORT holds up the first letter)

VILLEFORT
What truth is there in the accusation contained in this letter?

EDMOND
None at all.

VILLEFORT
Did you ever serve under the usurper Napoleon Bonaparte before his exile?

EDMOND
I did not.

(VILLEFORT picks up the package)

VILLEFORT
This was found in your quarters on board the Pharaon. Tell me of it.

EDMOND
Yes sir. LeClere, the captain, took ill during our voyage, and died of fever. On his death bed he ordered me to make for Elba, and to receive a package there, bound for Paris. He begged me to make sure this package reached its destination. It was the command of a superior officer, and a dying man's last request. Surely you can understand that.

VILLEFORT
And to whom were you instructed to deliver this package?

EDMOND
To a Monsieur Noirtier.

VILLEFORT
What was that name?

EDMOND
Noirtier. Do you know him? Monsieur de Villefort?

VILLEFORT
Did you examine the contents of this package?

EDMOND
No. It was not my place.

VILLEFORT
I see. Tell me, do you know what Providence is?

EDMOND
Sir?

VILLEFORT
Providence is the will of God. It was Providence that brought you before me today.

EDMOND
What do you mean?

VILLEFORT
Edmond Dantès, I am not able to restore you to liberty as soon as I had hoped. You should, from this point on, avoid dwelling on what might be. You will surely go mad. *(VILLEFORT exits)*

EDMOND
But I was to be married today. There must be something you can do. Her name is Mercedes. You can at least tell her where I am. Please. Monsieur de Villefort! Her name is Mercedes. Mercedes!

(The JAILERS enter and drag EDMOND away)

SCENE FIVE

(Lights shift to Albert's apartment in Paris. The apartment contains a painting of a young MERCEDES, dressed as a fisher-woman, looking out at the sea. ALBERT enters with EUGENIE)

EUGENIE
And where does this mysterious Count come from?

ALBERT
Really, I don't know. We were in Rome when I met him three months ago. Who knows where he may have gone in that time.

EUGENIE
And he told you three months ago that he would meet you here, in your parlor, today, at precisely ten o'clock in the morning? Is anyone capable of being so exact?

ALBERT
I think him capable of anything.

EUGENIE
And where is the fabled Monte Cristo, of which this

man is lord and master?

ALBERT
It is an island. A grain of sand in the middle of the Mediterranean. I'm told that smugglers use it, but honest sailors have no reason to land there unless they have a taste for goat.

EUGENIE
Goat?

ALBERT
Apparently that's all the island has to offer. Goats, and, somewhere, a cave filled with gold and jewels.

EUGENIE
Your Count keeps his fortune in a cave? How very Arabian Nights of him.

ALBERT
The cave, I admit, is a fantasy on my part. But everything else about the man is so exotic, I would almost be disappointed if he didn't have a cave full of treasure somewhere.

(The clock starts to chime)

EUGENIE
Ten o'clock, Albert.

(EDMOND enters on the tenth chime)

EDMOND
Punctuality, I've heard it said, is the politeness of kings. I hope you will excuse my two or three seconds' tardiness; five hundred leagues are not to be accomplished without some trouble.

ALBERT
My dear Count! Eugenie, this is the very man I've been

telling you about. Monsieur le Comte, I have the honor to present to you one of my oldest, dearest friends, Mademoiselle Eugenie Danglars.

EDMOND
Mademoiselle.

EUGENIE
Five hundred leagues, Monsieur? Do you often travel fifteen hundred miles just for a social visit?

EDMOND
It depends on who I'm visiting. But I delight in the exhilaration of speed, and my horses are bred to order.

ALBERT
You see? And he talks like that all the time!

EDMOND
But tell me, is not your father the Baron Danglars?

EUGENIE
He is, your excellency. Do you know him?

EDMOND
I know of him, and I expect to make his acquaintance soon.

ALBERT
Really? Do you play the markets, Count?

EDMOND
When it suits me. But tell me: I recollect that when the viscount and I were in Rome there was some talk of a projected marriage. May I congratulate you?

ALBERT
Not yet. But my father is most anxious about it.

EDMOND
Well, I imagine it is the nature of parents to be anxious

about such things. *(Referring to the painting)* This is... impressive.

ALBERT
Do you like it?

EDMOND
Very much. Reminiscent of a young Leopold Robert, but not quite... My dear viscount, you don't strike me as a man of artistic aspirations.

ALBERT
And you would be correct. What you see there is an original work of one Eugenie Danglars.

EDMOND
Truly?

EUGENIE
Albert's mother asked me to paint it for her, as a gift to the Count de Morcerf.

EDMOND
It's one of the finest I've seen. I shall commission a painting of my own from you.

ALBERT
Count, that's not really—

EUGENIE
It would be my privilege, Count.

EDMOND
This really is extraordinary. No doubt your father treasures it, Albert.

ALBERT
Oddly enough, this portrait seems to displease him for some reason. But between ourselves, my father may be a respected peer and renowned general, but his under-

standing of art is mediocre at best. So, I keep it here. You will do me the favor, Count, of making no allusions to this picture when you meet my parents. It seems to have a malign influence. My mother rarely looks at it without weeping.

EDMOND
You may rely upon me.

(FERNAND enters)

ALBERT
Ah! I have the honor of presenting the Count of Monte Cristo, the generous friend I was so fortunate to meet in Rome. My father, the Count de Morcerf.

FERNAND
You are most welcome, monsieur. My wife will be along shortly, to thank you herself, but allow me to say that you have rendered our house a service which insures you our eternal gratitude.

EDMOND
It is a great honor to me, on my first day in Paris, to meet a man whose merit equals his reputation, General. I have read with great interest all about your service to the late Pasha of Yanina.

FERNAND
Yes, well, I only wish those events concluded in a more favorable outcome.

EDMOND
Truly. The Pasha was a great man, by all accounts.

(MERCEDES enters. She freezes in the doorway)

ALBERT
And this is my mother, the Countess. Mother, this is the

Count of Monte Cristo.

MERCEDES
I've been waiting to meet you for so long, monsieur. I owe my son's life to you, and I'm grateful for the opportunity to thank you. It is very fortunate for my son that he found such a friend.

(EDMOND bows)

MERCEDES
Forgive me, but you seem so familiar to me. Surely we've met somewhere before?

EDMOND
I don't see how, madame, as this is my first time in France.

FERNAND
Well, Count, my wife is hosting a ball next week, and you certainly must do us the honor of attending.

(ALBERT and EUGENIE make sounds of agreement)

EDMOND
You are most generous, but the hostess has not invited me.

ALBERT
But of course she would want you there. Tell him, mother.

MERCEDES
Yes, of course. Please come.

EDMOND
I look forward to it. Well, I am most grateful for your kindness, but I got out of my travelling carriage at your door this morning. I must go and see what sort of lodgings have been procured for me.

EUGENIE
You haven't seen your own house yet? Where is it?

EDMOND
I believe I have it... Here it is. Number 30, Champs Elysees.

ALBERT
Never before in Paris, and you have a house in the Champs Elysees? You obviously have some genie at your control.

EDMOND
Spread that idea. It will be worth something to me among the ladies. *(To EUGENIE)* And I do hope you will indulge me in what I hope will be the first of many lengthy conversations about painting.

EUGENIE
I look forward to it.

EDMOND
Excellent. Good day.

(EDMOND shakes hands with FERNAND and exits)

MERCEDES
Albert, what sort of name is Monte Cristo?

ALBERT
Just a title, I believe. The Count purchased an island, and named himself after it.

EUGENIE
His manners are perfect, at least as far as I could judge in the few minutes he was here.

MERCEDES
Do you think the Count is really what he appears to be?

ALBERT
Why? What does he appear to be?

MERCEDES
He seems... a man of distinction. And we have every reason to show him our gratitude. But Albert, be prudent.

(MERCEDES and FERNAND exit)

ALBERT
Well, there you have it. I knew he would create a sensation here, and if mother is struck by him he must indeed be remarkable.

(ALBERT and EUGENIE exit)

Scene Six

(Lights shift to the street outside the Danglars' home. EDMOND and BENEDETTO enter. CADEROUSSE appears in the background, spying on them)

EDMOND
This is the place. Benedetto?

BENEDETTO
Yes, Count?

(EDMOND hands a slip of paper to BENEDETTO)

EDMOND
Here is the telegram. Be sure it arrives at precisely—

BENEDETTO
A quarter past. I know it.

EDMOND
Good. Meet me here when it's done.

(BENEDETTO takes the telegram and exits. Lights shift to the office of BARON DANGLARS, who sits at his desk, writing in a ledger. He looks up as EDMOND enters)

EDMOND
Baron Danglars.

DANGLARS
Ah! So good of you to call. My daughter Eugenie could talk of nothing else last night but mysterious Count of Monte Cristo.

EDMOND
I had the opportunity to view one of your daughter's paintings. She is quite gifted.

DANGLARS
Yes, well, we all must have our little hobbies, no?

EDMOND
Indeed. Well, down to business, Baron. I believe by now you should have received a letter from my agent in Rome, allowing me to open up a line of credit with you in Paris.

DANGLARS
Yes, well, Monsieur—That is to say—

EDMOND
I trust everything is correct? You did receive the letter?

DANGLARS
Oh, yes, but, ah… Well, the letter gives you unlimited credit.

EDMOND
Yes?

DANGLARS
The word "unlimited," in financial affairs, is extremely vague.

EDMOND
It is, in fact, unlimited.

DANGLARS
Could I have some indication of the amount you propose to draw?

EDMOND
I have no idea. If I knew I would not need unlimited credit, would I?

DANGLARS
Of course.

EDMOND
Listen sir, if you are unable to provide the funds I require, I have letters for some of the other banking houses here in Paris—

DANGLARS
No no! I am, of course, prepared to provide you with—

EDMOND
Good, fine. Be kind enough, then, to send me, oh, five hundred thousand francs in cash tomorrow. You may leave it with my steward if I'm not home. Good day, Baron.

DANGLARS
Count! Forgive me. I had thought I was acquainted with all the great fortunes in Europe, but this is the first I've heard of yours. May I presume to ask how long you have possessed it?

EDMOND
It has been in the family a long while, a sort of treasure expressly forbidden to be touched for a certain number of years. It only came available recently.

DANGLARS
I see.

EDMOND
I imagine I appear as something of an enigma to you, Baron. Don't worry; you will be better informed about me before long.

(HERMINE enters. She carries a telegram)

HERMINE
Oh, excuse me. I didn't realize that my husband had business this morning.

DANGLARS
Ah. Yes. My dear, allow me to present the Count of Monte Cristo. He has been warmly recommended to me. Count this is my wife, the Baroness Hermine Danglars.

EDMOND
Madame.

HERMINE
Ah! Of course. My daughter Eugenie speaks quite highly of you. She says you have arrived just yesterday from the extreme end of the globe. Is this true?

EDMOND
Not this time. I have merely come from Cadiz.

HERMINE
You have selected a most unfavorable time for your first visit, I'm afraid. Paris is a horrible place in the summer. I do hope you found suitable lodgings.

EDMOND
Suitable enough for me. I am at Number 30, Champs Elysees.

HERMINE
Number... 30, was it?

DANGLARS
I say, I know that house. My dear, wasn't it in your family for a time?

HERMINE
It was. A long time ago.

EDMOND
Really? How extraordinary. You must do me the honor of paying a visit. I wonder if you will find the place much changed.

HERMINE
That sounds... lovely.

EDMOND
Well, if you will excuse me. Baron, this has been most satisfactory. Good day. Madame.

(EDMOND *exits. DANGLARS returns to his desk, placing Edmond's letter in a book. HERMINE stares off*)

DANGLARS
Yes? ... Hermine? ... Baroness?

HERMINE
Yes?

DANGLARS
Was there something you wished?

HERMINE
Oh. Yes. This telegram just arrived for you.

(DANGLARS *takes the telegram and reads it*)

DANGLARS
Well. It appears I shall have to sell off the Spanish funds, and quickly. *(Noticing that* HERMINE *is distracted)* Are you all right?

HERMINE
What? Yes. I'm fine. Did you say you were selling the Spanish funds?

DANGLARS
Yes.

HERMINE
That can't be right.

DANGLARS
I pay good money for this information. It has never led me wrong before. Are you sure you're all right?

HERMINE
Yes. I'm just going to lie down for a bit. Let me know what happens with this.

DANGLARS
Of course, dear.

(HERMINE and DANGLARS exit separately)

Scene Seven

(Lights shift to the street outside Danglars' office. BENEDETTO enters. CADEROUSSE enters behind him)

CADEROUSSE
Pardon me if I disturb you, friend. May I speak with you?

BENEDETTO
Begone, sir. You have no right to beg here.

CADEROUSSE
I am not begging, my fine fellow. I only wish to say two or three words.

BENEDETTO
What do you want? Speak quickly.

CADEROUSSE
I want you to take me up in your fine carriage and carry me back to town, Master Benedetto.

BENEDETTO
What did you call me?

CADEROUSSE
Please don't think I want the glory of riding in your fine carriage. It's only because I'm tired, and also because I have a little business to talk over with you.

BENEDETTO
Who are you?

CADEROUSSE
Don't remember me? You wound me, Master Benedetto. All the time we spent together at the Pont du Var, before the prison ship sailed. And then there I was, chained to an oar, and you were nowhere to be seen. What could have happened to my dear friend Benedetto? I wondered.

BENEDETTO
I warn you, Caderousse, that you are mistaken.

CADEROUSSE
Ah, and here I worried that you might not recognize me. And look at you, with a carriage, and fine new clothes. You must have discovered a mine, or else become a stockbroker.

BENEDETTO
What do you want?

CADEROUSSE
I want to know about all this. It is a blessing when good fortune happens to friends.

BENEDETTO
It's no business of yours. It's a... a family matter.

CADEROUSSE
That friend of yours, the one you were talking to just now. He looks rich.

BENEDETTO
You want money?

CADEROUSSE
Not much. Enough to live... comfortably. In exchange, I promise not to spoil whatever game you have going with this fellow.

BENEDETTO
Fine. Tell me where to find you.

CADEROUSSE
Ah, no. I know what happens to your friends when they get on your bad side. Why do you think I waited till you were out in public before approaching you? I'll find you. I think five hundred a month should be sufficient.

BENEDETTO
Fine. Now get out of sight.

CADEROUSSE
Until our next meeting, Benedetto.

(CADEROUSSE exits. EDMOND enters)

EDMOND
Well done.

BENEDETTO
It arrived then? The telegram?

EDMOND
It did. You routed it properly?

BENEDETTO
Everything as you said. It should look just like it came from Spain.

EDMOND
Who was that?

BENEDETTO
Just some beggar. How did it go with the Baron?

EDMOND
Everything is on schedule. Fetch the carriage.

BENEDETTO
When do we see Villefort?

EDMOND
Fetch the carriage.

BENEDETTO
Yes, Count.

(BENEDETTO exits. EDMOND watches him leave, then looks back toward where CADEROUSSE exited)

EDMOND
Right on schedule.

(EDMOND exits)

Scene Eight

(Lights shift to Haydee's chamber in Edmond's home. HAYDEE is getting ready for the ball. There is a knock at the door)

EDMOND
Haydee?

HAYDEE
Yes?

EDMOND
(Off) May I enter?

HAYDEE
You may.

(EDMOND enters)

HAYDEE
Why do you always ask permission?

EDMOND
Haydee, you know that we are in France now.

HAYDEE
Of course.

EDMOND
You know that by law no person on French soil can be a slave. Here you are absolute mistress of your actions. You may go abroad or remain in your apartments, whatever seems most agreeable to you. You can go anywhere, see anyone. You are free.

HAYDEE
Free to do what?

EDMOND
Anything. Whatever you wish.

HAYDEE
You know what I wish.

EDMOND
I do.

HAYDEE
It's your wish too.

EDMOND
It is.

HAYDEE
Then why would I want to see anyone else?

EDMOND
It's almost time. Are you sure you want to do this?

HAYDEE
Will he be there?

EDMOND
Of course. It's his house.

HAYDEE
Then I'm sure. I have to know for certain. What of Benedetto?

EDMOND
What of him?

HAYDEE
You like to think of me as a daughter; doesn't that make him your son? We are a family of sorts. But he's still new to this. He needs a careful hand.

EDMOND
I will look after him as best I can.

(HAYDEE takes EDMOND's hands)

HAYDEE
And what of you? What do you need?

EDMOND
Haydee, I could be your father.

HAYDEE
You could be. You aren't. The love I have for you is very different from the love I had for my father.

(EDMOND ignores the question)

EDMOND
Are you ready?

HAYDEE
I am.

(EDMOND offers HAYDEE his arm, which she takes. They exit)

Scene Nine

(Lights shift to the home of the Morcerfs. ALBERT, EUGENIE, HERMINE, DANGLARS, FERNAND, and MERCEDES are all present, along with a SERVANT who continually enters and exits with trays of food. EDMOND, HAYDEE and BENEDETTO appear, away from the main group. Everyone is dressed in their finest for the ball)

BENEDETTO
I look like a buffoon.

EDMOND
A rich buffoon. Once more, are you certain you are ready?

HAYDEE
Yes.

BENEDETTO
Let's just get this over with.

EDMOND
Then follow me.

(EDMOND, HAYDEE, and BENEDETTO enter the party)

ALBERT
The Count of Monte Cristo!

EDMOND
Your humble servant, as ever, Albert. It's good to see you.

ALBERT
You remember Eugenie?

EDMOND
Of course.

ALBERT
Do you know how many people have asked about you? Seventeen. That's just here, tonight. But I can assure you that the Count of Monte Cristo is the only thing anyone is talking about, from the cafes to the opera houses.

EDMOND
Give it a month. Something new will come along.

ALBERT
Only a month? Well, I shall have to enjoy this celebrity-by-proximity while I can.

EDMOND
How goes your painting?

EUGENIE
Very well, thank you, Count. In fact, I was just—

(DANGLARS steps in between ALBERT and EUGENIE, interrupting)

DANGLARS
Count, so good to see you again.

EDMOND
Baron Danglars, just the man I hoped to see. I have the privilege of presenting His Excellency, Count Andrea Cavalcanti, newly arrived from his estates in Italy. Count, the Baron and Baroness Danglars.

DANGLARS
Your Excellency.

(BENEDETTO shakes DANGLARS' hand)

HERMINE
Excellency.

(BENEDETTO takes HERMINE's hand and bends over it, about to kiss it)

BENEDETTO
Madame. *(He kisses HERMINE's hand)*

EUGENIE
Albert, who is that?

ALBERT
That would be the Count's Greek slave. To be honest, I don't think I've ever heard her name.

EUGENIE
Slave? He can't take that too seriously, bringing her to France.

ALBERT
I don't think he does. The rumor is that he paid for her to save her from a worse fate.

EUGENIE
She's lovely.

(EDMOND draws BENEDETTO away from the DANGLARS)

EDMOND
If you will pardon us, Count, there are some friends I would like you to meet. *(Quietly, to BENEDETTO)* Focus. The hardest part is done.

BENEDETTO
I'm fine.

EDMOND
Prove it.

(EDMOND walks BENEDETTO over to ALBERT and EUGENIE. He raises his voice to be heard by the guests)

EDMOND
Count, this is the young man I told you about. Albert, the Count here is eager to hear about your adventures in Rome. The name Luigi Vampa is famous all over Italy, and they are always hungry for new tales of his exploits.

DANGLARS
Ah, Monsieur de Monte Cristo, may I have a word?

EDMOND
Of course, Baron.

(EDMOND leaves BENEDETTO with ALBERT and EUGENIE)

DANGLARS
Who is this gentleman?

EDMOND
You heard. His name is Cavalcanti.

DANGLARS
Yes, but I'm afraid I—

EDMOND
Of course! I imagine you know little of the Italian nobil-

ity. The Cavalcanti are all descended from princes.

DANGLARS
Has he any fortune?

EDMOND
An enormous one.

DANGLARS
What does he do?

EDMOND
Tries to spend it. Indeed, I invited him here because I thought you and he might do business together.

DANGLARS
And what brings him to Paris?

EDMOND
I believe he intends to marry, Baron.

DANGLARS
Marry whom?

EDMOND
Whomever he chooses, I would imagine. There is no shortage of likely candidates.

(MERCEDES approaches EDMOND)

MERCEDES
Count, Albert tells us that your home is extraordinary. I cannot believe you only bought it a week ago. I seem to recall that it stood empty for some time.

EDMOND
Twenty years, or so I was told. The garden required the most work, but I am fond of my grass and shade.

EUGENIE
It hasn't been occupied for as long as I can remem-

ber. It was always quite melancholy to look at, with the blinds closed and the doors locked, and the weeds in the courtyard. Do you remember, Albert? We made up stories about how the house was cursed, and that horrible crimes had been committed there.

EDMOND
The same idea crossed my mind the first time I saw it.

HERMINE
And yet you chose to stay?

EDMOND
Who can account for taste? The walls seemed to me to breathe sadness, and I thought I might stay a while and breathe it with them. The windows themselves seem to look down and say, "We have seen." Of course, you can imagine my shock when I discovered that they weren't lying.

HERMINE
No.

EDMOND
Oh yes. As incredible as it may seem, it is my opinion that a crime has been committed in my house.

FERNAND
Careful, Count. You'll frighten the ladies.

EUGENIE
Mother? Are you all right?

HERMINE
Of course. It's nothing. Do go on, Count.

EDMOND
There has been a crime. I had the earth in the garden dug up and fresh mould put in. While digging, my men

uncovered the broken remnants of a box, in the midst of which was the skeleton of a newly born infant.

FERNAND
Really, Count. This story is too much—

HERMINE
How do you know it is a crime?

EDMOND
How is it not a crime to bury a living child in a garden?

HERMINE
Living?

EDMOND
If it were already dead, why bury it there? A garden is no cemetery.

BENEDETTO
I wonder, what is done to infanticides in this country?

DANGLARS
Oh, their heads would be promptly cut off.

BENEDETTO
Indeed?

HERMINE
I'm sorry, I must... I must...

FERNAND
See, Count? I told you, you would frighten the ladies.

HERMINE
I must go. Please fetch the carriage. *(HERMINE exits)*

DANGLARS
Of course, dear.

(DANGLARS and EUGENIE follow)

Scene Ten

(Lights shift to the gate in front of the Morcerfs' home. HERMINE enters, gasping for air. EUGENIE enters a moment later)

EUGENIE
Mother? Are you all right?

HERMINE
I'm fine, dear. I just need some air.

EUGENIE
Was the Count's story really that frightening?

HERMINE
He is... a vivid storyteller. Where is your father?

EUGENIE
Fetching the carriage.

HERMINE
Eugenie, please give my apologies to Albert and his family. I'm just going to take a ride to collect myself. Go on, dear. It's over now, and I'm feeling better already.

EUGENIE
You're sure?

HERMINE
I am. The carriage is coming. You go on ahead.

(EUGENIE exits. HERMINE waits until she's gone, then exits in another direction)

Scene Eleven

(Lights shift back to the party. MERCEDES and EDMOND meet)

EDMOND
Madame, may I complement you on a lovely home and a splendid affair.

MERCEDES
I just hope the Baroness will be all right.

EDMOND
I'm sure she'll be fine.

(The SERVANT approaches with a tray of finger foods, which EDMOND waves off. The SERVANT exits as EUGENIE enters)

EDMOND
(To EUGENIE) Ah, Mademoiselle! *(To MERCEDES)* Madame. *(EDMOND moves off to speak with EUGENIE)* Tell me, when Albert spoke of your painting and the effect it had on his parents, what did you think?

EUGENIE
Honestly, Monsieur, I saw it as a complement. I believe the Count and Countess de Morcerf do not have the happiest of marriages. There is a sadness to the Countess that she hides from everyone. I don't think the Count or even Albert could see it. Perhaps it is not what the Countess wanted me to capture in her portrait, but the truth is I can only paint what I see.

(The SERVANT makes another approach, which EDMOND again waves off. Across the room, MERCEDES approaches ALBERT)

MERCEDES
Did you notice that?

ALBERT
What, mother?

MERCEDES
The Count will partake of no food in this house. I have watched him.

ALBERT
So?

MERCEDES
I should like to have seen the Count take something. *(MERCEDES raises her voice to be heard by the room)* Monsieur de Monte Cristo. *(The room stops to listen to MERCEDES)* I think we would all prefer to breathe in the garden rather than suffocate here. If you would oblige me with your arm, Count, I will lead the way.

(Pause. EDMOND offers his arm to MERCEDES, who takes it. They exit, followed gradually by everybody else)

Scene Twelve

(Lights shift to a secluded part of the garden. MERCEDES and EDMOND enter alone)

MERCEDES
Do you know where I am leading you?

EDMOND
No, madame. But you see I make no resistance.

(They pass a grapevine. MERCEDES takes a bunch)

MERCEDES
Albert tells me you've spent a great deal of time in Sicily. Our French grapes cannot compare, I know, but you must make allowance for our northern sun. *(She offers the grape to EDMOND, who does not take it)* Do you refuse?

EDMOND
Pray excuse me, madame, but I never eat Muscatel grapes.

MERCEDES
Really. You know, Count, there is a beautiful Arabian

custom which makes eternal friends of those who have eaten bread and salt together under the same roof.

EDMOND
I know it, madame. But we are in France.

MERCEDES
We are friends, though. Are we not?

EDMOND
Certainly, we are friends. Why shouldn't we be?

(MERCEDES does not answer. They continue walking)

MERCEDES
That young and lovely woman. She is your wife?

EDMOND
She is a slave, madame. I bought her at Constantinople.

MERCEDES
There is no one else then?

EDMOND
Once, at Malta, I loved a young girl, was on the point of marrying her, when war came and carried me away. I thought she loved me well enough to wait for me, but when I returned she was married. This is the story of most men who have passed twenty years of age, I know. Perhaps my heart was weaker than most men, and I suffered more than they would have done in my place. Who can say?

MERCEDES
And did you ever see her again?

EDMOND
Never. I never returned to the country where she lived.

MERCEDES
To Malta?

EDMOND
Yes, Malta.

MERCEDES
Do you still hate her?

EDMOND
Hate her? Not at all. Why should I? *(Silence)* Forgive me, madame. It grows late. I must take my leave.

(MERCEDES offers the grapes again)

MERCEDES
Take some.

EDMOND
Madame, I never eat Muscatel grapes. Good night.

ALBERT
Mother?

MERCEDES
I'm here, Albert.

ALBERT
Is everything all right?

MERCEDES
Fine. What is it?

ALBERT
The guests are asking for you.

MERCEDES
Of course.

(They exit)

Scene Thirteen

(Flashback. Lights shift to EDMOND in his cell at the Chateau d'If)

EDMOND
I want to know what crime I have committed. To be tried, and if I am guilty, to be shot; if innocent, to be set free. Sometimes, in my voyages, I would see the heavens overcast, the sea rage and foam, the storm arise and, like a monstrous bird, beat the horizon with its wings. Soon the fury of the waves and the sight of the sharp rocks announced the approach of death, and death then terrified me. I used all my skill and intelligence as a man and a sailor to struggle against the wrath of God. But I did so because I was happy; because I had not courted death; because I was unwilling that I, a creature made for the service of God, should serve as food for the gulls and ravens. But now it is different. I have lost all that bound me to life. I die after my own manner. I die exhausted and broken-spirited. Death smiles and invites me to repose.

(The ABBE FARIA'S voice comes from offstage)

FARIA
Who talks of God and despair at the same time?

EDMOND
What?

FARIA
That sounds like the voice of a young man. What is your name?

EDMOND
I am... Prisoner Number Thirty-Four. Who are you?

FARIA
I am Prisoner Number Twenty-Seven. Is your jailer gone?

EDMOND
Yes. Where are you?

FARIA
A moment, and you shall see.

(Some bricks in the wall of EDMOND's cell fall away, and out crawls ABBE FARIA)

FARIA
This is unfortunate. I have obviously dug in the wrong direction.

EDMOND
Who are you? How did you come here? Did you think to escape? How would you get off the island?

FARIA
Slowly, my son. We have all the time in the world for questions. I am the Abbe Faria. I have been imprisoned here in the Chateau d'If for ten years. I have spent much of that time thinking over all the most celebrated cases

of escape on record. They have rarely been successful.

EDMOND
Ten years? Have you been digging that whole time?

FARIA
Of course not. I spend most of my time studying.

EDMOND
Studying? But they allow no books—

FARIA
I had nearly five thousand volumes in my library at Rome. After reading them over many times I found that with one hundred fifty well-chosen books, a man possesses all that man really needs to know. I devoted three years of my life to reading these one hundred fifty volumes until I knew them nearly by heart, so that since I have been in prison a very slight effort of memory has enabled me to recall their contents as though the pages were open before me.

EDMOND
The guards speak of a prisoner here, a priest, who offers a fortune in gold and jewels to anyone who will help him off the island. They say he is…

FARIA
Mad? I suspect I am that fellow. I have been accused of it often enough.

EDMOND
Do you really have a hidden treasure?

FARIA
Whatever answer I gave you, would you believe it? But tell me, what is your name, and what brings you here, my young friend?

EDMOND
My name is Edmond Dantès. How I came here I never knew. I was accused of possessing some sort of package, which somehow made me a supporter of the usurper, Napoleon Bonaparte. The crown prosecutor told me it was nothing, a mistake, but I have been here for six years.

FARIA
Six years is a long time to be a mistake.

EDMOND
You don't believe me?

FARIA
I didn't say that. But I suggest to you that, guilty or not, no one comes to the Chateau d'If by mistake. Is there anyone to whom your disappearance could have been useful?

EDMOND
No one. I was a very insignificant person.

FARIA
Your reply employs neither logic nor philosophy. Everything is relative, from the king who stands in the way of his successor, to the employee who keeps his rival out of a job. What were you before?

EDMOND
I was about to become captain of a ship. I was about to marry a beautiful girl.

FARIA
Could anyone have had any interest in preventing the accomplishment of these things?

(EDMOND does not answer)

FARIA
Ah. There is someone. And by your look I imagine you thought of him as a friend.

EDMOND
There were two of them. Fernand and Danglars. I remember. I saw them... the day before I was arrested...

FARIA
Were they alone?

EDMOND
No. There was a third person, a man I knew by sight, named Caderousse. How strange that it should not have occurred to me before.

FARIA
Well now, is there anything else I can assist you in discovering, besides the villainy of your friends?

EDMOND
I... I wouldn't presume—

FARIA
Presume away, my boy. We have all the time in the world. It will be another ten years, at least, before we can dig our way to the sea from here. Although it is more likely that I'll find the usual way there long before then.

EDMOND
The usual way?

FARIA
I'm old, Edmond. One of these days, probably sooner than later, they will wrap me in a winding sheet and throw me over the cliff wall into the sea. No guest of the Chateau d'If has ever departed by any other means. *(Taps his head)* Thankfully, I have books enough to keep me occupied between now and then.

EDMOND
Will you teach me some small part of what you know?

FARIA
Teach you?

EDMOND
If only to prevent your growing weary of me. I can well believe that so learned a person as yourself might prefer solitude to—

FARIA
My boy, I only worry that we will run out of subjects. There is only so much I have to teach. Once you have mastered mathematics, physics, history, philosophy, literature, art, Latin, Greek, and the four or five modern languages with which I am acquainted, you will know as much as I do myself.

EDMOND
When can we begin? What shall you teach me first?

FARIA
Everything.

Scene Fourteen

(Lights shift to a street outside Danglars' office. BENEDETTO enters, escorting EUGENIE)

BENEDETTO
I, too, am a musician, or at least my tutors used to tell me so. But I found that my voice was not suited for music. What was it you played again? Piano?

EUGENIE
I paint, Monsieur Cavalcanti.

BENEDETTO
Delightful!

EUGENIE
You do know, Monsieur, that the viscount Albert de Morcerf is a regular guest here. He is a dear friend of mine.

BENEDETTO
I completely understand.

EUGENIE
What is it you understand, Monsieur?

(DANGLARS enters and observes)

BENEDETTO
Dearest Eugenie, though I am a prince, and the difference between our stations makes me fear to offend you by speaking of my love, yet I cannot find myself in your presence without longing to pour forth my soul, and tell you how fondly I adore you. If it be but to carry away with me the recollection of such sweet moments, I could thank you even for chiding me, for it leaves me a gleam of hope that at least I was in your thoughts.

(Pause)

EUGENIE
Right. Thank you for a most... entertaining walk, Monsieur Cavalcanti, but now I must wish you a good evening.

BENEDETTO
Mademoiselle Eugenie, will you at least give me a sign that I am in your thoughts, if not yet in your heart?

EUGENIE
Why not? *(EUGENIE exits)*

DANGLARS
Are you not rather young, Monsieur Andrea, to think of marrying?

BENEDETTO
I think not, sir. In Italy the nobility generally marry young. Life is so uncertain that we ought to secure happiness while it is within our reach.

DANGLARS
But how is it that your patron, Monsieur de Monte Cristo, did not make the proposal for you?

BENEDETTO
The Count is, doubtless, a delightful man, but inconceivably peculiar in his ideas. He has declared that he has never taken the responsibility of making proposals for another, and he never would. But he will answer any questions you may have for him.

DANGLARS
Well. If the Count of Monte Cristo speaks for you, who can speak against?

BENEDETTO
May I hope, sir?

DANGLARS
Commend me to your patron, won't you?

BENEDETTO
Of course.

(They exit separately)

Scene Fifteen

(Lights shift to Edmond's home. ALBERT enters. EDMOND enters a moment later)

EDMOND
Albert! Good morning. To what do I owe the pleasure of your company today?

ALBERT
You're in a good mood.

EDMOND
And why not? Aren't you?

ALBERT
Honestly, Count, I can't decide. I don't know whether to be cross with you or thank you.

EDMOND
To what do you allude?

ALBERT
To the installation of my rival at the Danglars'.

EDMOND
Rival?

ALBERT
I refer to your protege, Count Andrea Cavalcanti.

EDMOND
Has he been paying his addresses to Mademoiselle Eugenie?

ALBERT
You should see the languishing looks he gives her, and he speaks in the most comical tones.

EDMOND
Why does this concern you? While the two of you are certainly good friends, there is no real spark between you and Eugenie. You said as much yourself. I thought you'd be relieved.

ALBERT
And I am, to a point. It's true, Eugenie and I have never really seen each other that way, but for some reason everybody else did, and I just thought that part of my life was decided. I assumed we would grow accustomed to each other, the way my mother and father are. Up til now I've always known what was expected of me, and I always knew that's what I would do. It never occurred to me that I'd have to figure out what to do next.

EDMOND
And Eugenie? What is her opinion of all this?

ALBERT
Ha. She'll barely notice when Cavalcanti is in the same room. She seems so unaffected by it all. I sometimes wonder if she has some secret plan to rid herself of the whole charade. I imagine it must be the artist in her. I'm

sorry, Count. I'm not in my usual spirits today.

EDMOND
My dear viscount, I have an infallible remedy to propose.

ALBERT
What is that?

EDMOND
A change. I had resolved to take a few days' respite from the city, and spend some time at my estates in Normandy. I am a sailor, at heart. I love the sea as a mistress, and pine if I do not often see her. I shall be happy if you will accompany me. Now, I have set some small business ventures in motion, and I must observe how they play out before I leave. But in a few days time I shall be entirely at your disposal.

ALBERT
That, Count, is the most splendid idea I have heard all day.

(ALBERT exits. EDMOND steps back to play both sides in a game of chess as his "business ventures" play out)

Scene Sixteen

(Lights shift to the home of Villefort. HERMINE and VILLEFORT enter together)

VILLEFORT
I wish you'd come to me sooner.

HERMINE
I tried. It's not as easy to get away from my family as it once was.

VILLEFORT
What exactly did this Count of Monte Cristo say?

HERMINE
I couldn't listen to it all. He had every detail exact, except...

VILLEFORT
Yes?

HERMINE
Gerard, he said the child had been buried alive. Why would he say that?

VILLEFORT
Did this man give any sign that he suspected you?

HERMINE
He didn't say anything directly, but can there be any doubt?

VILLEFORT
Without evidence there is nothing but doubt.

HERMINE
But how can you explain it? It was all as he said, right there, in the very same house.

VILLEFORT
You say he has business with your husband? Is it possible that the Baron is finally putting his foot down?

HERMINE
You know he'd never do that. He's willing to be cuckolded so long as he can use my family's connections to boost his social standing. *(VILLEFORT laughs)* You find that amusing?

VILLEFORT
I find it pathetic, actually. But also practical.

HERMINE
You could at least act jealous.

VILLEFORT
Of the Baron Danglars? He's little more than a toy to you.

HERMINE
Perhaps, but he does have a gift for attracting money.

VILLEFORT
Not lately. Some error of judgement involving Spanish funds?

HERMINE
A telegram from a normally trustworthy source provided bad information. The timing could not be worse. Monte Cristo has already withdrawn over a million. My husband has had to call in some debts to cover it. You hear everything, don't you?

VILLEFORT
If it's worth knowing, yes.

HERMINE
And yet you've heard nothing about this man.

VILLEFORT
On the contrary, I ordered a report on the Count of Monte Cristo as soon as he appeared in Paris. The accounts of his exploits would make a fine novel. He arrived here from the south of Spain barely a week ago. Before that he was in Florence, then Rome. His title is from Tuscany, but the man himself is English, according to one source, Italian to another, and yet another places his origin somewhere in the Far East. His business dealings span the continent from London to Constantinople and trace back to the purchase of the island of Monte Cristo ten years ago. And before that...

HERMINE
What?

VILLEFORT
Before that, nothing. There is no record of this man. He doesn't exist.

HERMINE
Gerard, he couldn't... Monte Cristo couldn't be telling the truth, could he? Because even after all this time, if I thought there was a chance our child had lived—

VILLEFORT
Hermine, there was no chance. I told you before. There was nothing you could have done.

HERMINE
I never even saw him. *(Pause)* Promise me something, Gerard. Monte Cristo. You'll take care of him, won't you?

VILLEFORT
Of course.

HERMINE
I'm afraid of him, Gerard.

VILLEFORT
Then I shall have to do something about it, shan't I?

(VILLEFORT pulls HERMINE in close)

HERMINE
Gerard, not here.

(HERMINE takes VILLEFORT's hand and leads him off)

Scene Seventeen

(Lights shift to Danglars' office. DANGLARS reads a newspaper. FERNAND enters)

DANGLARS
Fernand, my old friend. To what do I owe the pleasure of this visit?

FERNAND
I thought it time we resumed our discussion.

DANGLARS
What discussion would that be?

FERNAND
You know very well. We were discussing a marriage between your daughter and my son. They are both old enough. I see no reason to wait any longer.

DANGLARS
Ah. Well, you will understand if I ask for a few days to reflect before I give you an answer.

FERNAND
What do you mean?

DANGLARS
I mean that it has been some time since we've spoken on this topic, and during that time unforeseen circumstances have occurred.

FERNAND
What circumstances?

DANGLARS
It is difficult to explain.

FERNAND
Let me be sure I understand you. I have come to remind you of our agreement. You fail to redeem the pledge. I have a right to an explanation, which you claim is "difficult." You decline to ally yourself to my family.

DANGLARS
I insist, I am not canceling our agreement. I merely delay it for a short time. During that time, I am certain, you will put these slanders to rest.

FERNAND
Who dares to slander me?

(DANGLARS *produces the newspaper.* FERNAND *takes it and reads*)

DANGLARS
It appears someone has taken an interest in your illustrious military career, Fernand. Questions about your time in Yanina? The Pasha? His wife and daughter? It's a shame none of them are still around to attest to your... loyalty.

FERNAND
What game is this?

DANGLARS
I believe we understand each other, Fernand.

(FERNAND throws the paper back at DANGLARS)

FERNAND
You of all people should know I am not a man to be trifled with.

DANGLARS
And you should know that the secrets we share would prevent me from spreading rumors about you in opposition newspapers. Nonetheless, I have a family to consider. Fix this, and we will talk. Eugenie and Albert are still young. We can afford to wait a few weeks.

(FERNAND storms out of Danglars' office. After he is gone, DANGLARS takes out the newspaper again and resumes reading)

DANGLARS
Very good.

(He continues reading as he exits)

Scene Eighteen

(Lights shift to the street outside of the home of Monte Cristo. BENEDETTO enters, followed by CADEROUSSE)

CADEROUSSE
Well, look at this place. I'm impressed.

BENEDETTO
How did you find me here, Caderousse?

CADEROUSSE
I followed you from the Danglars'. This game grows more interesting all the time. The Baron and I go way back, you know. I'd watch out if I were you, Benedetto. He's not as warm and cuddly as he seems.

BENEDETTO
I sent the money last week, just like you asked.

CADEROUSSE
You sent a servant. Wouldn't come and see your old friend yourself. Hurt my feelings, Benedetto.

BENEDETTO
What do you want? More money? That is one thing I have more than enough of.

CADEROUSSE
Wrong. That is one thing your benefactor, the Count of Monte Cristo, has more than enough of. But what if you should fall out of his favor? What would become of me?

BENEDETTO
We'd be in the same boat.

CADEROUSSE
Your fall would be a bit farther than mine, I think. But not to worry. I've thought it all out. What I need is a nest egg. This little game you have going? I want in.

BENEDETTO
You can't be serious.

CADEROUSSE
Why not?

BENEDETTO
This... game... is above your league.

CADEROUSSE
What, play-acting and dressing fancy? Oh, you're right. I've never gone in much for that.

BENEDETTO
It's beyond that. This is personal. I told you before, this is a family matter.

CADEROUSSE
You are not going to tell me that Monte Cristo is your long-lost father, or something ridiculous like that, are you?

BENEDETTO
No, not him—

CADEROUSSE
I don't care, Benedetto. I tell you what. I'll keep it simple. You just let me know when your friend the Count is away from home, and I'll stop by and clean house a bit. What do you say?

BENEDETTO
You're mad.

CADEROUSSE
And you need me to keep quiet, Count Andrea Cavalcanti.

(Pause)

BENEDETTO
Tonight. He'll be at the opera with his Greek girl.

CADEROUSSE
Tonight. See you then, Benedetto.

(They exit separately)

SCENE NINETEEN

(Lights shift to Edmond's drawing room. ALBERT enters with a copy of the same newspaper DANGLARS was reading. EDMOND stops his chess game to join ALBERT)

EDMOND
Albert? What is it?

ALBERT
I am to fight today. In the cause of honor. I come to beg you to render me a service. Will you be my second?

EDMOND
Slow down. With whom are you going to fight?

ALBERT
Read for yourself.

(ALBERT hands the newspaper to EDMOND, who reads it over)

EDMOND
"It has long been believed that the castle of the Pasha

of Yanina fell to the Turks after a brutal attack, and that the Pasha himself was killed in the defense of his citadel at the end of the Greek and Turkish war. However, new evidence has come to light which implicates the French general Fernand Mondego, the Count de Morcerf, in the final surrender."

ALBERT
You see? My father was the Pasha's chief military advisor. This swine seeks to claim that he had a hand in his death. That he betrayed the Pasha, whom he had sworn to protect.

EDMOND
This article suggests your father committed treason.

ALBERT
You understand now why I must fight. I inherit my father's name, and I do not choose that the shadow of disgrace should darken it. I am going to find the editor of this journal and I shall insist on his retracting the assertion.

EDMOND
And if he will not?

ALBERT
Then he must fight. I ask you again: Will you be my second?

EDMOND
No.

ALBERT
No? How can you object?

EDMOND
I do not say that you ought not fight; I only say that a duel is a serious thing, and ought not to be undertaken without due reflection.

ALBERT
Did this man reflect before he insulted my father?

EDMOND
Suppose the assertion to really be true.

ALBERT
No son ought submit to such a stain on his father's honor.

EDMOND
Listen to me. This... editor... whoever he is, is not your enemy. No, hear me out. This is a man who works in some cramped office, his back stiff from leaning over a desk, his fingers stained with years of ink. What's he to your father, or your father to him? Your enemy is not this man, who did nothing but print words in a paper. You must look deeper. Consider: these events took place what, sixteen, seventeen years ago? It is no accident that this comes to light now. You must find the source of these words.

ALBERT
But how?

EDMOND
Not by picking fights with random newspaper editors. Whoever planted this story would not leave a trail for you to find that way. Be prudent. You cannot flush this enemy out. Not yet. But if you are patient, he will make his next move.

ALBERT
And then?

EDMOND
Then you will know the truth. And you will be able to act accordingly.

(ALBERT exits)

Scene Twenty

(BENEDETTO enters, and is surprised to find EDMOND waiting)

BENEDETTO
You're home?

EDMOND
How did things go with the Baron?

BENEDETTO
Fine. I thought you were taking Haydee to the opera?

EDMOND
As you can plainly see, that is not the case. I am expecting a visitor. What's the matter, Benedetto? You seem on edge.

BENEDETTO
I'm fine.

EDMOND
Good. Tell me about Danglars.

BENEDETTO
It went just as you said it would. The man is still suspicious, but he's getting desperate. Between the money you keep drawing from him on one end and the bad investments on the other, he should be penniless in a month.

EDMOND
Very good. Was there something else?

BENEDETTO
Villefort. There's been no sign of him.

EDMOND
No. Not yet.

BENEDETTO
We had an agreement.

EDMOND
And I will uphold my end, so long as you uphold yours.

BENEDETTO
Why toy with them?

EDMOND
You'd prefer a knife through the ribs? Quick and painless, just like that?

BENEDETTO
You think I'd let it be painless?

EDMOND
I think you could never make it painful enough. You've come with me this far. I've brought you this close. Let me bring you all the way. Remember where I found you. A convict, half starved, on your way to the guillotine. And you deserved it. What, are you going to deny it? Now? To me? Have you forgotten so soon?

BENEDETTO
I haven't forgotten. But you shouldn't forget, either. Don't forget what I'm capable of.

EDMOND
On the contrary, I'm counting on it.

(During EDMOND and BENEDETTO's conversation, CADEROUSSE breaks in through an upstairs window)

EDMOND
Ah. That would be Monsieur Caderousse.

BENEDETTO
Caderousse—!

(EDMOND cuts him off with a wave. He signals to BENEDETTO, who nods and exits. CADEROUSSE sneaks into the room where EDMOND is waiting for him)

EDMOND
Good evening, Monsieur Caderousse. I knew you would make your way to me eventually.

CADEROUSSE
The Count of Monte Cristo, I presume? Did Benedetto tell you I was coming?

EDMOND
He didn't have to. Your whole life has been leading you to where you stand right now.

CADEROUSSE
Your voice is familiar. Have we met somewhere before?

EDMOND
Gaspard Caderousse, I offer you now a chance at absolution.

CADEROUSSE
Are you alone, sir?

EDMOND
I am.

CADEROUSSE
The worse for you, then.

(CADEROUSSE draws a knife and attacks EDMOND. EDMOND easily disarms CADEROUSSE, knocking him back. During the struggle, BENEDETTO re-enters, unseen, carrying a knife of his own)

CADEROUSSE
Who are you?

(BENEDETTO stabs CADEROUSSE in the back. CADEROUSSE collapses)

BENEDETTO
I had to. He would have ruined everything.

EDMOND
Very likely. Monsieur Caderousse could always be counted on to do anything but the right thing.

BENEDETTO
How did you know?

(ALBERT calls from offstage)

ALBERT
Count?

EDMOND
Get out. Now.

(BENEDETTO exits)

ALBERT
Count? Are you home?

EDMOND
Albert? Is that you? In here! Quickly!

(ALBERT enters)

ALBERT
I'm sorry it's so late, but I—What happened?

EDMOND
I found him senseless at the gate when I arrived home. He appears to have been stabbed.

ALBERT
Did anyone see it?

CADEROUSSE
Benedetto... Benedetto...

ALBERT
Benedetto? Is that who attacked you?

EDMOND
Albert, I need you to go find help while I tend to his wound. Can you do that?

ALBERT
Of course.

EDMOND
Hurry!

(ALBERT exits)

CADEROUSSE
You... Benedetto...

EDMOND
Silence. God in his mercy has given you these few extra moments that you might reflect and repent.

CADEROUSSE
Who are you? I know you...

EDMOND
Yes, Caderousse. You knew me once. You may not have written the letter that condemned me, but your inaction helped to fasten my chains. A word from you could have fixed everything, but you chose silence. And now I stand before you, rich, happy, and safe while you lie in utter despair. Look. Look at my face. Do you know what Providence is?

CADEROUSSE
You. It's you. Oh. Oh God.

(CADEROUSSE dies. EDMOND slips a folded piece of paper into CADEROUSSE's jacket)

EDMOND
That's one.

END OF ACT ONE

ACT II

Scene Twenty-One

(Lights up on EDMOND, seated in his opera box. Below lies CADEROUSSE's corpse, covered with a sheet. EDMOND holds up a jewel to the light. Two GENDARMES enter and remove CADEROUSSE's body. EDMOND holds up a second jewel. DANGLARS enters, working furiously at a ledger. He compares figures from telegrams with his own, tears them in frustration. DANGLARS exits. EDMOND holds up a third jewel. FERNAND enters. He is attempts to place a badge of office on himself, and notices that the badge is tarnished. He tries to wipe it clean, but fails. EDMOND holds up a fourth jewel, and MERCEDES enters. She approaches FERNAND and moves to take the badge from him, but he recoils and exits. MERCEDES exits. EDMOND holds up a fifth jewel, and VILLEFORT enters. EDMOND closes his hand around the jewels and exits the opera box)

Scene Twenty-Two

(Lights shift to Edmond's drawing room, where VILLEFORT paces. EDMOND enters)

EDMOND
Magistrate, forgive me for making you wait.

VILLEFORT
Monsieur le Compte, we meet at last.

EDMOND
Was this meeting predestined?

VILLEFORT
I only mean that I have heard nothing but "Monte Cristo" for the last few weeks, and have been anxious to meet such a celebrity. I only wish it could be under more pleasant circumstances.

EDMOND
Hmm.

VILLEFORT
It is also my privilege to inform you that I will be personally overseeing this investigation.

EDMOND
Is it the practice in Paris for the king's prosecutor to investigate every vagrant who dies in the street?

VILLEFORT
In the street? No. But on the property—indeed, in the parlor—of so distinguished a gentleman as yourself...

EDMOND
I understand. I hope you will find myself and my household entirely at your disposal. May I ask if you have any leads?

VILLEFORT
Your friend, the viscount de Morcerf, has stated that the victim mentioned the name, "Benedetto." We found a note in the corpse's pocket that sheds some light on this. Are you familiar with the name?

EDMOND
I'm afraid not.

VILLEFORT
May I ask, Count, what brings you to Paris?

EDMOND
I came here to continue my studies.

VILLEFORT
And what do you study?

EDMOND
My fellow man. I have sought to make a physiological study of the human race. My method requires extensive travel, as I believe it would be easier to descend from the whole to a part, rather than ascend from a part to the whole. It is an algebraic axiom which makes us proceed from a known to an unknown quality, and not from unknown to known. If you take my meaning.

VILLEFORT
Ah. Philosophy. Forgive me, but if, like yourself, I had nothing but idle time, I should seek a more amusing occupation.

EDMOND
Nothing but idle time? Let me ask you, sir: Do you really believe that you have anything to do? Do you believe that what you do deserves to be called anything?

VILLEFORT
I understand you have spent a good deal of time in the Orient. Perhaps you are not aware that human justice, while so expeditious in barbarous countries, in France requires a prudent and well-studied course.

EDMOND
True, but I have found that the law of primitive nations to be closer to the law of God. Perhaps this will be the law in France one day.

VILLEFORT
Perhaps. But until then our codes are in full force, with all their contradictory enactments derived from Gallic customs, Roman laws, and Frank usages. And the moment you become an inhabitant of France, you become subject to its laws.

EDMOND
I know it, sir. But you will forgive me when I say that your "justice" holds no particular terror for me.

VILLEFORT
And why is that?

EDMOND
As happens to every man once in his life, I have been

taken by Satan to the highest mountain on earth, and there he showed me all the kingdoms of the world, and he said to me, "Child of earth, what wouldst thou have to make thee adore me?" I reflected long on this before I replied. "I have always heard of Providence, and yet I have never seen him, nor have I seen that which can make me believe he exists. I wish to be Providence." Satan bowed his head and groaned. "You mistake, Providence does exist. You have never seen him because he moves by hidden ways. I cannot make you Providence, but I can make you one of his agents." The bargain was concluded. I may lose my soul, but what does that matter? If the bargain were offered again I would not change it.

VILLEFORT
I confess, Count, this the most stimulating conversation I've had for some time. I do hope we can continue it soon.

EDMOND
I look forward to it. Please keep me apprised of your investigation.

VILLEFORT
Of course, Monsieur. Before I go, may I ask one more question?

EDMOND
If you think it will help.

VILLEFORT
This house, sir. What made you purchase it?

EDMOND
The garden. There is none like it in all of Paris. Would you care to see it?

VILLEFORT
Another time, perhaps. Adieu, sir.

(VILLEFORT exits, passing ALBERT as he enters)

ALBERT
Was that Monsieur de Villefort, the king's prosecutor?

EDMOND
It was. It appears he has taken a personal interest in the case. I have decided to be flattered by the attention. But how are things with you?

ALBERT
Impatient. You've seen the papers?

EDMOND
I have. It appears these rumors about your father are not going to fade on their own.

ALBERT
You should have seen the looks I was getting at the opera the other night. I must ask you, do you still counsel me to wait?

EDMOND
I do. I know it won't be easy for you, but any action you take right now will only fan the flames of this scandal. In the meantime, I suggest you find more pleasant ways to occupy your time.

ALBERT
Such as?

EDMOND
Joining me for dinner this evening. Perhaps Eugenie could accompany us.

ALBERT
Haven't you heard? Baron Danglars has decided to marry

Act Two

Eugenie to Andrea Cavalcanti.

EDMOND
Has he now? How does that sit with you?

ALBERT
I don't believe Eugenie will be happy with this match.

EDMOND
You think she'd prefer you?

ALBERT
I think she'd prefer to make her own choice.

EDMOND
Will you hear a little advice?

ALBERT
From you, always.

EDMOND
Eugenie can take care of herself. You will see.

ALBERT
That I do not doubt.

EDMOND
I have thought of a better idea than dinner. I believe our trip to Normandy cannot wait a moment longer. A few days' rest at the seashore will do us both a world of good.

ALBERT
You still want to go?

EDMOND
It is needed now more than ever. How soon can you be ready?

ALBERT
I am prepared to leave today, if you like.

EDMOND
Perfect. Shall we?

(EDMOND and ALBERT exit)

SCENE TWENTY-THREE

(Flashback. Lights shift to EDMOND in a cell as FARIA joins him. The hole dug by FARIA is visible)

FARIA
Tell me, what has hindered you from tearing a leg from this stool, knocking down your jailer with it, dressing yourself in his clothes, and endeavoring to escape?

EDMOND
I suppose it never occurred to me.

FARIA
Because the natural repugnance to the commission of such a crime prevented you from thinking of it. Man loathes the idea of blood. His natural construction inspires him to shrink with dread at the thought of taking a life. What are you thinking of?

EDMOND
I was reflecting upon the enormous degree of intelligence you must have employed to reach such a high level of perfection. What would you have accomplished

if you had been free?

FARIA
Possibly nothing at all. In a state of freedom the overflow of my brain might have evaporated in a thousand follies. Misfortune is needed to bring to light the treasures of the human intellect. Captivity has brought my mental faculties to a focus. But I think there was another subject in your thoughts.

EDMOND
Not at all.

FARIA
There is a clever maxim which states that unless wicked ideas take root in a naturally depraved mind, human nature, in a right and wholesome state, revolts at crime. You, my friend, were thinking about the third man in your triumvirate.

EDMOND
Villefort.

FARIA
Indeed. So, your shipmate Danglars wished to be captain ahead of you. He knew of this package from Elba, and he found common interest in the love-struck Fernand. But the deputy prosecutor. What motive could he have had? What are your thoughts?

EDMOND
I have none. I've been over and over it. He didn't know me, had no reason to hate me, or want me out of the way.

FARIA
What do you know of this Villefort?

EDMOND
Very little. He was a prominent official. He made a name

for himself pursuing Napoleon's agents, but he had a reputation for fairness.

FARIA
He hunted the Emperor's agents? That is interesting. I knew of a Villefort some years ago who was a fearsome supporter of Napoleon. Noirtier, his name was.

EDMOND
What did you say?

FARIA
Noirtier de Villefort. He fought for Napoleon against the Royalists. Why Edmond, what is it?

EDMOND
The package from Elba. I was instructed to deliver it to Paris. To a Monsieur Noirtier.

FARIA
Edmond, tell me. The crown prosecutor. What was his full name?

EDMOND
Gerard de Villefort.

FARIA
Oh Edmond, Edmond. How simple it all is. Gerard de Villefort is Noirtier's son. See how it all falls into place? His own father was still active on behalf of the Usurper, and you were the one person in France who could prove it. If the younger Villefort was as ambitious as you say, he had no choice but to send you away, or risk his father's discovery and his own disgrace.

EDMOND
Will you excuse me? I must have time alone to think over all of this.

FARIA
Ah. Now there is a look I know well. I fear I shall come to regret having helped you in this line of inquiry.

EDMOND
Why?

FARIA
Because it has instilled a new passion in your heart. Vengeance.

(FARIA and EDMOND exit)

SCENE TWENTY-FOUR

(Lights shift to the Danglars' home. HERMINE, EUGENIE, and BENEDETTO enter. They are all dressed for a formal event.)

HERMINE
Eugenie, darling, we have a hundred guests downstairs, waiting for this contract to be read. You could at least stand a little straighter for my sake. That dress would look lovely on you if only you didn't slouch so. Don't you agree, Count?

BENEDETTO
Oh, never will such a complaint escape from my lips. Heaven keep me from jesting with that which is far dearer to me than life itself.

EUGENIE
What excessive nonsense you do talk, Monsieur.

HERMINE
Eugenie!

EUGENIE
Forgive me. I must have a word with my father before we begin this... proceeding.

(EUGENIE exits)

HERMINE
I'm sure she's just nervous, Count. I don't mean to keep plucking at her, but she is my only child, after all. Surely you understand.

BENEDETTO
Surely.

(Lights shift to Danglars' office, where DANGLARS goes over the details of the contract. DANGLARS is also dressed for the occasion. EUGENIE enters)

EUGENIE
Father, I must speak to you.

DANGLARS
I will be happy to speak with you when this business is concluded.

EUGENIE
It is precisely "this business" that I wish to discuss. Let me be plain: I will not marry Count Andrea Cavalcanti.

(DANGLARS stops reading the contract)

DANGLARS
My dear, why are you unhappy now?

EUGENIE
Unhappy? Since this little affair began I have not manifested the slightest opposition, even though you well know that I have never held my tongue when things displease me. I proceeded from a wish to be an obedient and devoted daughter. I tried to the very last and

now that the moment has come I find that in spite of all my efforts it is impossible.

DANGLARS
What's wrong with him? Do you find him disagreeable? Is he ugly?

EUGENIE
I am sure that Monsieur Cavalcanti is a perfectly adequate specimen of his kind.

DANGLARS
Please do not tell me it's because you aren't in love with him.

EUGENIE
That is quite beneath me, father; I am no schoolgirl. The truth is that I love no one, sir, and I do not see why I should encumber my life with a perpetual companion. I would rather cast this useless encumbrance into the sea and remain with my own will, disposed to live perfectly alone, and perfectly free. I'm told I am beautiful, witty, talented, and rich—and you have taught me that last is its own kind of happiness—so why do you call me unhappy?

DANGLARS
Dearest daughter, I believe I understand your sentiments. Now, if you will allow me to clarify a few things, particularly in regard to this notion of being "rich."

EUGENIE
Please do.

DANGLARS
You admire candor, and I hope you will be satisfied. I did not propose that you marry Monsieur Cavalcanti for your sake. Indeed, I did not think of you in the

least. I made this arrangement because it suited me to marry you off as soon as possible, on account of certain commercial speculations into which I intend to venture.

EUGENIE
I see.

DANGLARS
To be blunt, this marriage is intended to save us from financial ruin. We were rich; we now stand on the precipice.

EUGENIE
How can that be?

DANGLARS
I would not presume to enter into arithmetical explanations with an artist like you. Just know that a banker's credit is his physical and moral life, and as his credit sinks, he becomes a corpse. And if you do not marry Monsieur Cavalcanti, they will be calling for the sexton and his spade. But when Cavalcanti signs the marriage contract he will place his fortune into my hands, amounting to fifteen million francs.

EUGENIE
How admirable.

DANGLARS
I would think you would be flattered, being valued so highly.

EUGENIE
I see. Well, you have explained yourself perfectly, sir. If I do not marry the Count, you are ruined. Let it be done, then. Let's sign the contract, and set the date for the wedding.

DANGLARS
That's it? What are you up to?

EUGENIE
Will you call them in, father, or shall I?

DANGLARS
(*Calling offstage*) We're ready.

(*BENEDETTO and HERMINE enter. DANGLARS makes a great show of the contract. He takes up a pen and prepares to sign*)

DANGLARS
I take great joy in this, and in you, whom I now call my son. With this contract, I secure our family's fortune. And my daughter's happiness.

(*VILLEFORT enters, armed*)

VILLEFORT
Monsieur Benedetto, you will come with me.

HERMINE
Gerard?

DANGLARS
What are you doing here, Villefort? Who is Benedetto?

VILLEFORT
He is. Benedetto, arrested for theft and murder, sentenced to the galleys, escaped confinement, and now charged with the murder of a fellow former prisoner, one Gaspard Caderousse, at the home of the Count of Monte Cristo.

DANGLARS
Caderousse? Did you say Caderousse?

VILLEFORT
I did.

DANGLARS
No, no, no. This isn't possible. Obviously there is some mistake.

(VILLEFORT produces the folded paper EDMOND slipped into CADEROUSSE's jacket)

VILLEFORT
We have the victim's own testimony. Benedetto, you will come with me.

(BENEDETTO draws his sword and grabs HERMINE, using her as a shield as he looks for an exit. HERMINE strikes him and gets away. VILLEFORT takes the opportunity and draws his sword. VILLEFORT and BENEDETTO fight. BENEDETTO injures VILLEFORT and escapes. Hermine rushes to VILLEFORT)

HERMINE
Gerard!

VILLEFORT
It's nothing. Are you all right?

(They realize that EUGENIE and DANGLARS are still in the room. HERMINE turns to EUGENIE)

HERMINE
Darling—

EUGENIE
Enough, Mother.

(EUGENIE exits)

HERMINE
Husband—

DANGLARS
Please, dear. Do not make this day any more embarrassing than it already is.

(DANGLARS exits)

VILLEFORT
I must go. Look to your family. We will speak soon.

(VILLEFORT exits, leaving HERMINE alone)

SCENE TWENTY-FIVE

(Lights shift to MERCEDES at the home of the Morcerfs. FERNAND enters, carrying a newspaper)

FERNAND
Mercedes.

MERCEDES
Fernand? I have not seen you home at this time of day in quite a while.

FERNAND
My dear, I must speak to you about a delicate matter.

MERCEDES
Yes?

FERNAND
It is nothing, I'm sure, but still I believe it must be addressed. These rumors about me. About my time in Yanina—

MERCEDES
I heard. They're saying awful things about you. That you

betrayed the Pasha, that you may have had something to do with his wife and daughter disappearing.

FERNAND
I swear to you, these are nothing but lies. But the damned press will not let it go. I must prepare a defense. The Senate has decided to call a hearing.

MERCEDES
Based on rumors? But you said there couldn't be any evidence against you.

FERNAND
No. Of course not.

MERCEDES
What could this mean?

FERNAND
Nothing. They have nothing.

MERCEDES
But if they did... If something happened, what would it mean for us?

FERNAND
It could be as simple as expulsion from the Senate, or...

MERCEDES
Or?

FERNAND
Or execution for treason.

MERCEDES
My God, Fernand.

FERNAND
I promise you, there is nothing to worry about. This is nothing. Just some political rival with a grudge. It will all be settled in the hearing.

MERCEDES
Fernand, you've never wanted to speak of your service to the Pasha, and I have always respected that. But I have to ask you—

FERNAND
Mercedes—

MERCEDES
Just help me understand why—

FERNAND
I don't wish to discuss it.

MERCEDES
Fernand, I never asked you because I didn't want you to have to lie to me. But if you are disgraced, or worse—

FERNAND
There is nothing worse.

MERCEDES
—then what happens to Albert? His whole life is built on your name. What happens then? I never asked for this. I was happy to remain a fisherman's wife, and raise Albert in our little village near Marseilles. We were happy there, remember?

FERNAND
I remember.

MERCEDES
Let me help you, Fernand. Whatever happened in Yanina, I know—

(FERNAND pulls away roughly)

FERNAND
Enough!

MERCEDES
Fernand, the well-being of our son is at stake. Why do you make me doubt you now?

FERNAND
Doubt?

MERCEDES
The Pasha had a family. A wife, and a daughter. Do you know what happened to them?

FERNAND
Madame, for the last time, I will not discuss this matter with you. Just know that all I have done—from here, to the Pasha's palace in Yanina, to our young days in Marseilles—was so that you might live in the manner you deserved.

MERCEDES
What does that mean, Fernand? What happened to the Pasha?

FERNAND
If you will excuse me, madame, I must prepare for my hearing. Good day.

(FERNAND exits)

MERCEDES
Fernand? What happened to the Pasha? Fernand!

Scene Twenty-Six

(Lights shift to the Danglars' home. DANGLARS enters, carrying traveling bags. HERMINE enters, catching him trying to leave)

HERMINE
What is this?

DANGLARS
Ah. Yes. Well, I suppose I owe you some explanation for my conduct. Our fortune is lost, I know not how. I can no longer put off my creditors. The wolves are at the door, and our last hope, a good marriage for our daughter, has failed us. I wonder, Hermine, if you admire the rapidity of my fall?

HERMINE
Admire it? Is this some last noble act of self-sacrifice I'm witnessing? If so, I'm afraid its meaning is obscure.

DANGLARS
I assure you, my dear, there is not one ounce of nobility here. What you see is strictly an exercise in

self-preservation.

HERMINE
And here I thought there were no surprises left between us.

DANGLARS
Give my regards to Magistrate de Villefort. He and I are old friends, after all.

HERMINE
He hates you.

DANGLARS
Of course he does. Did he ever tell you why?

HERMINE
Isn't it obvious?

DANGLARS
Don't flatter yourself. The good magistrate had bigger secrets than you.

HERMINE
I know all about his father, if that's what you mean.

DANGLARS
He told you about the infamous Noirtier de Villefort? There was a time when dear Gerard would have locked you up for the rest of your life just to keep that information secret. Amazing. I suppose he must actually love you.

HERMINE
My God, you are grotesque.

(During the following, EUGENIE enters and overhears. She is also packed to travel)

DANGLARS
In earlier days I philosophically closed my eyes, because

I thought at least your efforts were meant to strengthen our house. You have no husband now. I imagine you might welcome that prospect, but I will not allow the ashes of my downfall to provide the foundation of another man's fortune. I have taken all that remains, and shall from this time forward labor only on my own account.

HERMINE
What about Eugenie?

EUGENIE
You needn't worry about me.

HERMINE
What are you doing? Go upstairs at once.

EUGENIE
Why? So you can try to marry me off again a month hence?

DANGLARS
Oh, let her go. No respectable family would come near her after this latest scandal.

EUGENIE
I did not seek this. I did not ask for it. But it has come, and I hail it joyfully.

(EUGENIE exits)

DANGLARS
Madame, I leave you with the same respect you have shown for me throughout our marriage.

(HERMINE slaps DANGLARS)

HERMINE
How strong and courageous you are.

(They exit separately)

Scene Twenty-Seven

(Lights shift to Edmond's seaside estate. EDMOND and ALBERT enter)

EDMOND
I am pleased you were allowed to join me here, Albert.

ALBERT
Allowed? I am a grown man. I may go where I please.

EDMOND
Even with the mysterious Monte Cristo?

ALBERT
You forget, Count. My mother has taken a deep interest in you. You must really be a very strange and superior man.

EDMOND
I suppose I have my moments.

ALBERT
My mother would have me draw you out, and find the heart of your mystery.

EDMOND
No doubt something else will catch her eye soon enough.

ALBERT
I think not. My mother speaks to me of little else.

EDMOND
And what does she say?

ALBERT
"Albert," she says to me, "I believe the Count has a noble nature. You must try to gain his esteem." You see then, instead of disapproving, she encouraged me to accompany you here.

EDMOND
Yes. Well, you will recall what Shakespeare said: "Woman is like a wave of the sea." I urge you to remember that.

(EUGENIE enters)

EUGENIE
Albert!

ALBERT
Eugenie? What are you doing here?

EUGENIE
Albert, listen to me. You must return home. Now.

ALBERT
Why? What has happened?

EUGENIE
Your father is accused of treason. The Senate has called for a hearing.

ALBERT
What?

EUGENIE
Your mother told me where to find you. I promised her I would tell you.

EDMOND
I'll have the carriage brought around. We'll depart at once.

(EDMOND exits)

EUGENIE
I'm so sorry, Albert.

ALBERT
I don't know what to do.

EUGENIE
Go to your mother. She needs you.

ALBERT
What about you? Where are you going?

EUGENIE
Italy, first. I've left my family, Albert. I'm going as far from Paris as I can get. A... a friend has provided me with letters of introduction. I'm going to study.

ALBERT
A friend? It's the Count, isn't it?

EUGENIE
He's an extraordinary man. I can't thank him enough for all he's done for me. But Albert...

ALBERT
What is it?

EUGENIE
The Count. Sometimes it's as though he's building some great machine, and we're all the cogs and wheels.

There is some motive behind his friendship. Don't you feel it?

(EDMOND enters)

EDMOND
The carriage is loading as we speak. We can leave whenever you wish, Albert.

EUGENIE
Goodbye, Albert. I hope we meet again.

(EUGENIE kisses ALBERT on the cheek, and takes the opportunity to whisper in his ear)

EUGENIE
Remember what I said. Be careful. *(To EDMOND)* Count.

EDMOND
My lady.

ALBERT
Goodbye, Eugenie.

(EUGENIE exits)

ALBERT
What now, Count?

EDMOND
The time has come. Your enemy has made his move. Soon you will know him, and you will act accordingly.

(They exit)

Scene Twenty-Eight

(Lights shift to the committee chambers. The CHAIRMAN and two PEERS take their places above. FERNAND stands below them. ALBERT finds a place in the back of the hall as FERNAND speaks before a committee)

FERNAND
My lords, the Pasha of Yanina had up to the last moment honored me with his entire confidence. I show you now the ring, the mark of his authority, which the Pasha gave to me, that I might at any hour, day or night, gain access to his presence. So great was his trust in me that I was chosen to represent him in negotiations that might have ended hostilities between his nation and the Turks. Unfortunately the negotiation failed, and when I returned to defend my benefactor, he was dead, and his wife and daughter disappeared. I have supplied Your Honors with documents and other proofs of my statement. In the absence of an accuser, I demand the libels against me be named as such, and those guilty

of spreading such falsehoods be punished.

CHAIRMAN
Is there a witness that will corroborate the statements published against the Count de Morcerf?

(HAYDEE enters. She wears the full regalia of an Ottoman princess)

HAYDEE
Your Honors, I can furnish this committee with important particulars regarding the conduct of the Count de Morcerf in this matter.

CHAIRMAN
Come forward, and state your business before this committee.

(HAYDEE moves to the witness stand)

FERNAND
What is this?

HAYDEE
I was there at the death of the Pasha of Yanina. I was present during his last moments. I know what became of his wife and daughter.

FERNAND
My lords, I have no idea who this girl—

CHAIRMAN
Mademoiselle, you claim to have been an eyewitness to this event?

HAYDEE
I was.

CHAIRMAN
But you must have been very young then.

HAYDEE
I was four years old, but not a single detail has escaped my memory.

CHAIRMAN
Who are you? And in what manner could these events concern you?

HAYDEE
I am Haydee, daughter and heir to the Pasha of Yanina.

FERNAND
My lords, please. How can anyone support such a claim?

CHAIRMAN
Can you prove the authenticity of your statement?

(HAYDEE produces documents)

HAYDEE
I can, sir. Here is the register of my birth, signed by my father and his principal officers. And this is of my baptism, my father having consented to my being brought up in my mother's faith.

CHAIRMAN
Monsieur de Morcerf, do you recognize this lady as the daughter of the Pasha of Yanina?

FERNAND
No. This is a base plot, contrived by my enemies.

HAYDEE
But I recognize you, Monsieur. You are Fernand Mondego, the French officer who led the troops of my noble father. It was you who betrayed him to the Sultan. And it was you who sold my mother and me to the slave merchants of Armenia. "Look well at that man," my mother said. "You had a beloved father. You were

destined to be a queen. Here is the man who raised your father's head on the point of a spear. Here is the man who sold us. Watch him close as the pieces of gold fall one by one into his hand."

FERNAND
This is hearsay, my lords.

CHAIRMAN
Young lady, what proofs do you offer?

HAYDEE
I have one last document to present, my lords. This is a bill of sale. Please note the signature, your Honors. My mother died in chains, and I was made a slave so that a French officer could gain four hundred thousand francs. I know him, my lords. Let him say he does not know me.

CHAIRMAN
Mademoiselle, how came you here?

HAYDEE
I was purchased again, sirs, seven years later, by the Count of Monte Cristo.

CHAIRMAN
Was it he, then, who counseled you to take this step?

HAYDEE
I was led to this step by my own grief. I have always sought to revenge my illustrious father. I have always known that the traitor lived in Paris, and since I set foot in France I have watched carefully. I am ignorant of nothing which passes in the world. This is a glorious day for me.

CHAIRMAN
Count de Morcerf, this is your signature, is it not?

Has the daughter of the Pasha spoken the truth? Speak, sir!

(FERNAND stares at HAYDEE for some time. Without acknowledging the CHAIRMAN or the committee, he exits. Chaos erupts. The CHAIRMAN tries to gavel the committee back to order, with no success)

CHAIRMAN
Count de Morcerf! Count de Morcerf! You leave us no choice! This committee moves to press charges of felony treason, and that a warrant be issued for your arrest!

(More chaos as the CHAIRMAN and PEERS exit. ALBERT runs up to HAYDEE, who has not moved. She does not acknowledge him. ALBERT exits. EDMOND enters. HAYDEE takes his hand and kisses it, then exits. EDMOND then takes his seat in the opera box and watches as the next scenes unfold)

Scene Twenty-Nine

(Lights shift to MERCEDES, in the Morcerfs' home. ALBERT enters)

MERCEDES
Albert! Have you come from the hearing? Is there any news—

ALBERT
Mother, I must ask you: Do you know if Monsieur de Morcerf has any enemies?

MERCEDES
"Monsieur de Morcerf"? You do not say, "my father"?

ALBERT
Does he?

MERCEDES
Albert, what has happened?

ALBERT
Mother, you recall on the evening of the ball we gave, you noticed that Monsieur de Monte Cristo would

not eat anything in our house.

MERCEDES
Why?

ALBERT
You know he has studied in the Orient, and it is customary there that one never eats or drinks in the house of an enemy.

MERCEDES
Albert, whatever idea you are entertaining, dispel it. Monsieur de Monte Cristo has only shown us kindness. He saved your life, and my counsel to you is to retain his friendship.

ALBERT
You have some special reason for wanting me to stay friends with him.

MERCEDES
Tell me what has happened.

(ALBERT moves to exit)

MERCEDES
Albert, I am not well. You should stay here and cheer my solitude. I do not wish to be left alone.

ALBERT
Mother, you know how gladly I would obey your wish, but an urgent affair obliges me to leave you for this evening.

(ALBERT bows to MERCEDES and exits. MERCEDES watches him go, then exits quickly in the opposite direction)

SCENE THIRTY

(Lights follow DANGLARS, still carrying his bags of money. He is lost, and tries to get his bearings on a map. LUIGI VAMPA enters)

LUIGI VAMPA
Baron Danglars. Welcome to Rome.

DANGLARS
What? How do you know my name?

LUIGI VAMPA
If you would be so good as to accompany me.

DANGLARS
Who are you?

LUIGI VAMPA
Luigi Vampa, at your service.

(LUIGI VAMPA aims a pistol at DANGLARS)

DANGLARS
No. You can't. Help! HELP! THIEF!!!

LUIGI VAMPA
Do not shame yourself, sir. I am not here to rob you. This is Italy, not France.

DANGLARS
I've heard well enough what happens here. How much do you require for my ransom? I can offer you one... one million francs.

LUIGI VAMPA
A million francs, you say? But you carry letters of credit totaling five million.

DANGLARS
How do you know that?

LUIGI VAMPA
That is not important. It is true, and that is all that matters.

DANGLARS
This is all the money I have left in the world. Why don't you take two million?

LUIGI VAMPA
Because what you ask is worth more than that.

DANGLARS
Three? Come, surely you cannot refuse three million?

LUIGI VAMPA
I can refuse it, and I do.

DANGLARS
Four million. I can't believe you've ever received such a ransom before.

LUIGI VAMPA
True, sir. But that still would not pay yours.

DANGLARS
Fine! Take it! Take it all!

LUIGI VAMPA
Keep your money, sir. You will need it.

DANGLARS
What do you mean? You aren't going to kill me?

LUIGI VAMPA
I am prohibited from shedding your blood, sir. I am to provide you with all of the services you may require. Are you hungry? Do you wish for some wine? Or water? You may have anything you desire. But I should warn you, our prices are extravagant.

DANGLARS
You won't allow me to purchase my freedom, but you expect me to pay for my food while you hold me captive? That is madness.

LUIGI VAMPA
That is the price of survival.

DANGLARS
And what happens when I have no money left to pay you?

LUIGI VAMPA
Then you will truly suffer.

(LUIGI VAMPA and DANGLARS exit)

Scene Thirty-One

(Lights shift to VILLEFORT. HAYDEE enters. Her face and clothing are hidden by a cape or cloak. She carries a note)

HAYDEE
Monsieur de Villefort?

VILLEFORT
Who are you?

HAYDEE
I have a message for you, from a friend.

VILLEFORT
And who is this friend?

HAYDEE
The Baroness Hermine Danglars.

VILLEFORT
Where is she?

(HAYDEE hands the note to VILLEFORT)

HAYDEE
She asks that you meet her here tomorrow night.

VILLEFORT
This... This is the home of the Count of Monte Cristo.

HAYDEE
Yes, Monsieur. The Baroness said you would understand the meaning.

(VILLEFORT exits. HAYDEE removes her covering and joins EDMOND in his opera box)

Scene Thirty-Two

(Lights shift to the Count's box at the opera. Neither EDMOND nor HAYDEE turn, or seem at all surprised, when ALBERT enters)

EDMOND
My cavalier has attained his object. Good evening, Monsieur de Morcerf.

ALBERT
I have not come here, sir, to exchange hypocritical expressions of politeness. I've come to demand an explanation.

EDMOND
At the opera?

ALBERT
We must avail ourselves of an opportunity whenever our object can be seen.

EDMOND
Where have you come from, sir? You do not appear to be in the possession of your senses.

ALBERT
I followed your advice. I waited for my enemy to reveal himself. He has. I am here. Do I make myself understood?

EDMOND
Mind your tone, Albert. People are starting to stare.

ALBERT
Let them.

EDMOND
It is in poor taste to make a display of a challenge, viscount. *(ALBERT raises up but EDMOND cuts him off)* You may consider your glove thrown, sir. Now leave, or I will summon my servants to throw you out the door. *(ALBERT again tries to speak and is cut off)* Pistols then. At eight o'clock. Now go home and go to sleep before you hurt yourself with all of your ill-chosen barbarisms.

(ALBERT exits. EDMOND escorts HAYDEE out)

Scene Thirty-Three

(Lights shift to the home of Monte Cristo. EDMOND and HAYDEE enter and find MERCEDES waiting)

EDMOND
Madame de Morcerf. How may I be of service?

MERCEDES
It is not Madame de Morcerf who comes to you. It is Mercedes, Edmond.

(EDMOND nods to HAYDEE, who exits)

EDMOND
What did you call me? I know no one of that name.

MERCEDES
Don't, Edmond. I knew you when I first saw you admiring my painting. I didn't speak because I thought you must have had good reason for hiding your true self. But after that night in my garden... I think you wanted me to know. And from that moment I have followed your steps, watched you, feared you. And I need not inquire which hand dealt the blow which now strikes Monsieur

de Morcerf.

EDMOND
Fernand, you mean? Since we are recalling names, let us remember them all.

MERCEDES
Spare my son, Edmond.

EDMOND
And who told you, madame, that I have any hostile intentions against your son?

MERCEDES
He attributes his father's misfortunes to you.

EDMOND
Madame, you are mistaken. They are not misfortunes. It is a punishment.

MERCEDES
And why do you represent providence? Why do you remember when it forgets? What is the Pasha of Yanina to you?

EDMOND
You are right; it does not concern me. All this is an affair between the French general and the Greek princess. I have sworn to revenge myself, not on the French general, or the Count de Morcerf, but on the fisherman Fernand, husband of Mercedes.

MERCEDES
Edmond, if you owe revenge to anyone it is to me. I did not have the fortitude to bear your absence and my solitude.

EDMOND
But why was I absent? Why were you alone?

MERCEDES
You were arrested, Edmond. You were a prisoner.

EDMOND
And why was I a prisoner?

MERCEDES
I don't know. I never knew.

EDMOND
Do you recall the night before our wedding? I had just arrived home from my latest voyage, and we held hands as we strolled through the streets of Marseilles. Do you remember? We passed an inn and saw our two dear friends, Danglars and Fernand, sharing a bottle of wine with old Caderousse. We called to them, but they didn't seem to hear.

MERCEDES
I remember.

EDMOND
They were busy composing this letter.

(EDMOND produces an aged letter, which he hands to MERCEDES)

EDMOND
Go on. Read it.

MERCEDES
"The king's attorney is informed by a friend to the throne and religion that one Edmond Dantès, second in command on board the Pharaon, this day arrived from Smyrna, is a bearer of a package from the usurper Napoleon Bonaparte to his agents in Paris. Should the package not be found with him, then it will assuredly be discovered in his cabin on board the Pharaon. Corroboration of this statement may be obtained by

arresting the above-mentioned Edmond Dantès."

(EDMOND takes the letter back)

EDMOND
It cost me two hundred thousand francs to track this down, but that is nothing. This resulted in my arrest. This ended my life, and you never knew. How could you have known that I remained within a quarter of a league from you, in a dungeon beneath the Chateau d'If, for fourteen years?

MERCEDES
Can it be?

EDMOND
It can, madame. All so that Danglars could earn the title of captain ahead of me—a title he would throw away just a few years later to become a banker. And all so that Fernand could replace me as your husband. They wrote this the night before our wedding and delivered it to the deputy prosecutor as Caderousse looked on and laughed. The next day all three of them stood silently in the church as the gendarmes dragged me from the altar and led me to my grave. But now I, betrayed, sacrificed, and buried, have risen from my tomb, by the grace of God, to punish them. He sends me for that purpose, and here I am.

MERCEDES
Forgive, Edmond. For my sake.

EDMOND
Impossible, madame.

MERCEDES
Edmond, why do you not call me Mercedes?

EDMOND
Mercedes. The name still has its charms. This is the first time in a long while that I have pronounced it so distinctly. Mercedes. I have uttered your name with a sigh of melancholy, with a groan of sorrow, with the last effort of despair. I have uttered it when frozen with cold, crouched on the straw in my cell. I have uttered it consumed with heat, lying on the stone floor of my prison. Fourteen years I suffered, I wept, I cursed, and now I tell you, Mercedes, I will have my revenge.

MERCEDES
Revenge yourself then, Edmond. But let your vengeance fall on the culprits—on Fernand, on me—but not on my son.

EDMOND
The sins of the father shall fall upon their children unto the third and fourth generation. Since God himself dictated those words, why should I seek to do any better?

MERCEDES
Edmond, since I first knew you, I have adored your name, have respected your memory. Edmond, my friend, do not compel me to tarnish that noble and pure image. If you only knew all the prayers I addressed to God for you while I thought you were living, and how many more since I thought you were dead. What could I do for you, Edmond, besides pray? Edmond, I swear to you, guilty as I was, I have suffered much.

EDMOND
Have you known what it is to see the woman you loved give her hand to your rival while you perish at the bottom of a dungeon?

MERCEDES
No. But I have seen him whom I loved on the point of murdering my son.

EDMOND
What would you say if you knew the extent of the sacrifice you ask of me? Suppose that God has paused in his work to spare an angel the tears that might one day flow for mortal sins from her immortal eyes; suppose that when everything was in readiness and the moment had come for God to look upon his work and see that it was good; suppose he had snuffed out the sun and tossed the world back into eternal night. Then, even then, Mercedes, you could not imagine what I lose in this moment. *(Pause)* Well. Let Albert live, then.

MERCEDES
Edmond. Though I no longer resemble my former self in my features, you will see that my heart is still the same. I have nothing more to ask of Heaven. I have seen you again, and found you as noble and as great as I always knew you were. Thank you, Edmond. Adieu.

(MERCEDES exits. HAYDEE enters)

HAYDEE
My lord? Everyone is talking of it. They say the affair is serious, and unavoidable. They say you are sure to kill him.

EDMOND
Do they. Haydee, I am going on a journey. If any misfortune should happen to me... I wish for you to be happy.

HAYDEE
You are going to spare him, aren't you.

EDMOND
I am.

HAYDEE
It is a matter of honor, my lord. Albert will kill you. He has to.

EDMOND
I know it.

HAYDEE
What has happened, my lord?

EDMOND
The same thing that happened to Brutus the night before the battle of Philippi.

HAYDEE
You have seen a ghost? And what did this ghost tell you?

EDMOND
That I have lived long enough. I have left my will upon the desk. My fortune is yours.

HAYDEE
Bequeath your fortune to others, my lord. If you die, I shall require nothing. I had but one purpose in my life. That purpose is fulfilled, and now the only thing that binds me to this earth is you.

EDMOND
Haydee—

HAYDEE
You have an appointment in the morning, my lord. I shall not keep you from it.

(HAYDEE exits. EDMOND watches her go, and then exits)

Scene Thirty-Four

(Lights shift to the home of the Morcerfs. ALBERT is leaving for the duel when MERCEDES stops him)

MERCEDES
Albert. Is it time already?

ALBERT
Soon, mother. I wished to be early.

MERCEDES
Of course. But you have a moment still. I want to tell you something before you go.

ALBERT
Mother, please do not—

MERCEDES
Just listen. After I've said what I wish you to hear, if you still must go, I won't try to stop you.

ALBERT
I asked you before what special reason you had that I should stay friends with this man.

MERCEDES
The story I wish to tell you is not about the Count of Monte Cristo. It is about a very different man, whom I knew before you were born. This man's name was Edmond Dantès.

(ALBERT and MERCEDES exit)

Scene Thirty-Five

(Lights shift to a wooded park, at dawn, present day. EDMOND enters, carrying pistols. He sets them aside, then kneels to pray)

EDMOND
I do this, O my God, as much for thy honor as for mine. I have for ten years considered myself the agent of thy vengeance, and other wretches, like Fernand, Danglars, and Villefort must not imagine that chance has freed them from their enemy. Let them know, on the contrary, that their punishment, which was decreed by Providence, is only delayed by my present determination, and although they escape this world, it awaits them in another, and they are only exchanging time for eternity.

(ALBERT enters)

EDMOND
Five minutes past, Albert. I would not have thought it of you.

ALBERT
Count... I...

EDMOND
You are not yourself, Albert. Is something wrong?

ALBERT
I must speak, sir.

EDMOND
Proceed.

ALBERT
Sir, I reproached you for exposing the conduct of my father, the Count de Morcerf, when he served in Yanina. Guilty though I knew he was, I thought you had no right to punish him. I have since learned that you had that right. It is not Monsieur de Morcerf's treachery toward the Pasha which induces me to excuse you, but the treachery of the fisherman Fernand Mondego towards you. I say, and I proclaim it publicly, that you were justified, and I thank you for not using greater severity. Now, sir, if you think my apology sufficient, please give me your hand. I acted well as a man, but you have acted better than a man. I hope the world will not call me cowardly for acting as my conscience dictated.

EDMOND
Providence still. Only now am I fully convinced of being the emissary of God.

ALBERT
Will you counsel me?

EDMOND
Of course, Albert.

ALBERT
What do I do now?

EDMOND
You are free, Albert. You can leave your father's house, leave Paris. Take your mother with you.

ALBERT
My mother?

EDMOND
You owe her more than you can ever pay her.

ALBERT
Where could we go? How will we live? I'm giving up all I have; I can't ask her to do the same.

(MERCEDES enters, unseen by EDMOND and ALBERT. She listens from the background)

EDMOND
Albert, listen. Once I was betrothed to a lovely girl whom I adored. With ceaseless toil I amassed a hundred and fifty louis. This money was for her, and I buried our little treasure in the garden behind a little house in Marseilles. Your mother, Albert, knew that house well. Not long ago I passed through Marseilles, and went to see the old place. It stands there still. In the evening I took a spade to the garden. The iron box was still there, under the fig tree my father planted on the day I was born. This money, Albert, was meant to provide comfort and tranquility to the woman I adored. Now, through strange and painful circumstances, it may still serve its intended purpose.

(MERCEDES steps forward)

MERCEDES
I accept it. Thank you, Edmond.

EDMOND
It was always yours, Mercedes.

ALBERT
Your work is done, then?

EDMOND
Not yet.

ALBERT
Count, I've asked you for advice many times, and you have never led me wrong. Let me repay you in kind.

EDMOND
I know what you will say. What you ask is impossible.

ALBERT
Even for the Count of Monte Cristo?

EDMOND
There is no Count of Monte Cristo but this.

ALBERT
Then I am sorry for you.

EDMOND
Perhaps you will allow me to visit you in Marseilles, when it is finished?

ALBERT
Goodbye, Count.

EDMOND
Goodbye, my friend.

(ALBERT and MERCEDES exit together. EDMOND watches them go, then exits)

Scene Thirty-Six

(Lights shift to the home of Monte Cristo. EDMOND enters to find FERNAND waiting for him)

EDMOND
Monsieur de Morcerf.

FERNAND
Did you not have a meeting with my son this morning?

EDMOND
I did.

FERNAND
And did my son not have good reasons to fight with you?

EDMOND
Yes, he had very good ones.

FERNAND
Doubtless you made some apology or explanation?

EDMOND
I explained nothing. Albert apologized to me.

FERNAND
And to what do you attribute this conduct?

EDMOND
To the conviction, probably, that there was one more guilty than I. I expected this result.

FERNAND
You expected my son would be a coward?

EDMOND
Albert de Morcerf is no coward.

FERNAND
A man who holds a mortal enemy within reach of his sword, and does not fight, is a coward! Why is he not here that I may tell him so?

EDMOND
Sir, I do not expect that you have come here to relate to me your little family affairs. I understand a warrant for your arrest will be issued today. I suggest that you state your business quickly.

FERNAND
I came to tell you that I also look upon you as my enemy. I came to tell you that I hate you instinctively; that it seems as if I had always known you, and always hated you; and, in short, since the young people of the present day will not fight, it remains for us to do so. Do you think so, sir?

EDMOND
Certainly.

FERNAND
Are you prepared?

EDMOND
I am.

FERNAND
Let us start, then. We need no witnesses.

EDMOND
Very true. It is unnecessary. We know each other so well.

FERNAND
Perhaps I may be more honorable in my shame than you under your pompous coverings. You call yourself the Count of Monte Cristo, but it is your real name I want to know, that I may pronounce it at the moment when I plunge my sword through your heart.

EDMOND
Do you not guess it, Fernand? Or rather, you remember it? For, not withstanding all my sorrows and tortures, I show you today a face which the happiness of revenge makes young again, a face you must often have seen in your dreams since the day you married my betrothed!

FERNAND
Edmond Dantès.

EDMOND
Fernand Mondego. What does your honor demand now?

(Stiffly, deliberately, FERNAND leaves EDMOND. Lights shift to the home of the Morcerfs as EDMOND exits. FERNAND encounters MERCEDES and ALBERT, who have their bags packed, on the steps. Pause)

ALBERT
Come, mother. This is no longer our home.

(ALBERT and MERCEDES exit. FERNAND watches

them exit, then proceeds to his office. From a drawer he produces a pistol. He loads it with meticulous care, then places the barrel at his temple, and fires)

SCENE THIRTY-SEVEN

(Lights shift to Abbe Faria's cell. FARIA sits alone, reading aloud from a book he made himself out of rags)

FARIA
"I am the Abbe Faria. I have been imprisoned in the Chateau d'If since the year 1811. During that year, destiny seemed subservient to every wish formed by Napoleon Bonaparte. Four years later this colossus of power would be overthrown, and the brother of the man he once deposed would reign in France. For what great and mysterious purpose has it pleased heaven to abase the man once so elevated, and raise up him who was once so abased? How inscrutable are the ways of Providence."

(FARIA suddenly goes rigid. The book slips from his fingers)

FARIA
Edmond! Edmond!

(FARIA collapses to the ground. Lights shift to Edmond's

garden, where HERMINE is seated. VILLEFORT enters)

VILLEFORT
Hermine?

HERMINE
Gerard? No, you must go...

(VILLEFORT moves to her and discovers she is covered in blood)

VILLEFORT
What? What happened?

HERMINE
Everyone is gone. I was alone. He came back and he took me. I'm sorry, Gerard. I'm so sorry.

VILLEFORT
Who did this to you?

BENEDETTO
(Off) Magistrate. Welcome home.

(Lights shift back to Faria's cell. EDMOND enters through the secret tunnel)

EDMOND
Abbe Faria? Father? Tell me what to do.

FARIA
Alas, Edmond, my dear friend. I do not need to explain this to you.

EDMOND & VILLEFORT
Help! Help!

FARIA
Silence! Or you are lost. Now believe me when I tell you that Providence does you a favor today. I am too old to be anything but a hindrance now.

EDMOND
Don't say that.

FARIA
Quiet now. Do you want the guards to discover all we've accomplished? Listen to me now. My son, I bless thee. I wish you all the happiness and all the prosperity you deserve. The treasure, the one the jailers claimed was a figment of my addled brain, is real. I see it now in the depths of a cavern. My eyes pierce the inmost recesses of the earth, and are dazzled at the sight of so much riches. You must go now, my son. And when you are out in the world again, hasten to Monte Cristo. Avail yourself of the fortune, for you have suffered long enough.

(EDMOND holds FARIA as the old man dies. As lights shift back to the Count's garden, EDMOND hides in the tunnel before JAILER 1 enters, finds FARIA's body and covers it with a sheet)

VILLEFORT
Benedetto?

HERMINE
He made me write to you, Gerard...

BENEDETTO
(Off) This garden. Do you find it much changed?

VILLEFORT
What?

BENEDETTO
(Off) You remember. This house was once owned by the Servieux family. Your family, madame. I never knew them, but I understand they were quite influential until a scandal nearly destroyed them. The rumor is that the daughter conceived a child out of wedlock. Shocking.

VILLEFORT
What do you want?

BENEDETTO
(Off) You know the story. Supposedly this daughter never revealed the identity of the scoundrel who disgraced her. In the end they had to marry her off to a young banker. I understand he's done quite well for himself since then. But the story never tells what happened to the baby.

VILLEFORT
It died.

(BENEDETTO appears behind HERMINE)

BENEDETTO
Did it.

(Lights shift to Faria's cell. EDMOND enters from the tunnel)

EDMOND
Father. For eight years I have learned from you. I speak five languages. I could recite the whole of Dante, Machiavelli, and Shakespeare. A world is open to me that I had not known existed. But if I am to enter this world, the time must be now. I can have everything, if I can just survive the fall. And so, Father, after all you have given me, I have one last boon to beg of you.

(EDMOND removes the sheet. He takes FARIA's body and hides it in the tunnel. Lights shift to the garden as EDMOND lies where FARIA had been, and covers himself with the sheet)

BENEDETTO
Do you recall a man named Bertuccio? Of course you don't. This man, Bertuccio, was a gardener. He worked here, for the Servieux family. He was here the night you

gave birth.

HERMINE
No.

BENEDETTO
You were upstairs. He was here. So were you, Magistrate.

HERMINE
No.

BENEDETTO
That gardener saw what you buried here.

HERMINE
The child was dead!

BENEDETTO
That child lived. Mother.

HERMINE
Lived! Our child... Gerard! How... You told me...

(BENEDETTO stabs HERMINE)

VILLEFORT
Hermine?

HERMINE
You told me... our child...

(HERMINE dies. Lights shift back to Faria's cell. The JAILERS enter)

JAILER 1
The madman has gone to look after his treasure. Good journey to him.

JAILER 2
All his millions, and yet he won't be able to pay for his shroud. Come on. Over the cliff with him.

(The JAILERS lift EDMOND and carry him out of the cell. Lights shift back to the Count's garden)

BENEDETTO
The gardener, Bertuccio, took me that night and ran. Even then he feared you. We lived as criminals, and it was easy enough to become one. One day when I cursed God for ordaining me to such a fate, Bertuccio said to me, "Do not blaspheme. The fault lies not with the Almighty, but with your father. Your father, who consigned you to hell." I have been a forger, a thief, and an assassin. And I am your son.

VILLEFORT
My son. Do you know what Providence means?

(VILLEFORT pulls a knife and stabs BENEDETTO. BENEDETTO falls to the ground. VILLEFORT drops the knife and goes to HERMINE. EDMOND enters. During the following, BENEDETTO manages to get hold of the fallen knife)

VILLEFORT
The agent of providence. Does this look like the will of God to you? Does it?

(EDMOND kneels by HERMINE's body)

EDMOND
No, it does not.

VILLEFORT
I have heard your voice before.

EDMOND
You heard it the first time at Marseilles, twenty-four years ago. I am the spectre of a wretch you condemned to the dungeons of the Chateau d'If. God gave that spectre this form when he issued from his tomb, enriched

him with gold and diamonds, and led him to you. Do you know me now?

VILLEFORT
I know you. I buried you. I buried both of you. Should I prostrate myself in terror, now that the dead have risen from their graves?

EDMOND
Not dead, Monsieur. Very much alive. And we will have justice.

VILLEFORT
Justice? Is that what this is? Your "justice" holds little terror for me.

EDMOND
Gerard de Villefort, I came to tell you that you have sufficiently repaid your debt, and that from this moment I will pray God forgive you.

VILLEFORT
Do not pray for me, Monsieur. My soul is stained, but at least it is my own, and I am prepared to answer for it. Can you say the same for yours? Look about you, Edmond Dantès. Are you well revenged?

(BENEDETTO *rises up and stabs* VILLEFORT *in the back.* VILLEFORT *falls dead next to* HERMINE. BENEDETTO *collapses.* EDMOND *draws close to him*)

EDMOND
Your mother thought you were dead, Benedetto. She was innocent in this.

BENEDETTO
Help me.

EDMOND
I saved you from the guillotine so that you might serve

my purpose, and in so doing, answer the crimes that were done to you. But I cannot absolve you of the crimes that you yourself committed. You became an instrument of divine retribution. Now, your purpose fulfilled, you are duly punished in your turn. I wonder, Benedetto, did it hurt as much as you hoped it would?

BENEDETTO
Please... help me...

EDMOND
Goodbye, Benedetto.

(EDMOND starts to walk away as BENEDETTO dies. ABBE FARIA enters, leading what appears to be a funeral procession. FERNAND and DANGLARS carry the stretcher bearing EDMOND's own covered body. MERCEDES follows, then ALBERT and EUGENIE, and HAYDEE. As they pass, VILLEFORT, HERMINE, and BENEDETTO rise up to join the procession. The living and the dead join their voices as they carry EDMOND to the cliff)

FARIA
Edmond, do you know what Providence is?

VILLEFORT
Who and what are you?

MERCEDES
Edmond.

VILLEFORT
Do you know what Providence is?

FARIA
Fourteen years.

VILLEFORT
I am unable to restore you to liberty.

FARIA
Now there is a look I know well.

MERCEDES
We were about to be married.

FARIA
It has instilled a new passion in your heart.

VILLEFORT
Do you know what Providence is?

FARIA
Vengeance.

VILLEFORT
Edmond Dantès, do you know what Providence is?

MERCEDES
The will of God.

FARIA
Vengeance.

MERCEDES
Providence.

VILLEFORT
You must avoid dwelling on what might be.

MERCEDES
Edmond!

FARIA
Do you know what Providence is?

ALL
It is the will of God.

(They throw EDMOND over the cliff)

Scene Thirty-Eight

(Lights up on DANGLARS, in the catacombs of Luigi Vampa's hideout. DANGLARS wears the same clothes he wore the last time we saw him, but they are completely filthy now. He is weakened with hunger and dehydration, but possesses a clarity, perhaps even wisdom, he lacked before)

DANGLARS
Is anyone there?

(He waits. There is no answer)

DANGLARS
Is anyone there?

(No answer)

DANGLARS
I would like some water, please. I... have nothing left to give. Nothing left. Please.

(No answer)

DANGLARS
I am being punished. And I... I accept it. But if I could only have some water. When I was first brought here I demanded my liberty. When I could not purchase that, I demanded comfort. Now, I only ask to live.

(EDMOND enters. DANGLARS does not see him, but he shows no surprise when he hears EDMOND's voice. DANGLARS accepts his fate now, whatever it is)

EDMOND
Do you suffer?

DANGLARS
I do.

EDMOND
Men have suffered worse than you.

DANGLARS
I know it.

EDMOND
Do you repent?

DANGLARS
I do.

(EDMOND moves to exit)

DANGLARS
Edmond Dantès.

(EDMOND halts)

DANGLARS
There was a man I knew. That was his name. I hated him. I can't... I can't remember why. It's strange. I haven't thought about him in so long. He has been on my mind more and more ever since I came here. For a time I

wondered what I would say, what I could say, if I ever saw him again. I know now. There is nothing. If Edmond Dantès stood before me, my life would end, and I would be glad to be rid of it.

(EDMOND exits silently, leaving the door open. After a time DANGLARS notices. He hesitantly examines the doorway, then exits)

Scene Thirty-Nine

(Lights shift to MERCEDES, who has changed to simple commoners' clothing. ALBERT enters, wearing the uniform of a common soldier)

ALBERT
Mother?

MERCEDES
Is it time already?

ALBERT
Soon. How do I look?

MERCEDES
It suits you. I wish it didn't—

ALBERT
Mother—

MERCEDES
—but I understand. I do.

ALBERT
Will you be all right when I'm gone?

MERCEDES
I believe I will. I grew up here. It's where I'm meant to be.

(EDMOND enters)

MERCEDES
Edmond?

ALBERT
Count? What are you doing here?

EDMOND
I'd gotten word that you had enlisted, and would soon be off to Africa.

ALBERT
You see it is true.

EDMOND
Quite a step down for the Viscount de Morcerf.

ALBERT
There is no Viscount de Morcerf. I am just Albert Mondego, the son of a fisherman.

EDMOND
I see.

ALBERT
Your work? It's finished?

EDMOND
It is.

ALBERT
Should I congratulate you?

EDMOND
I wanted to ask, Albert, if you would care to come with me.

ALBERT
Come with you? Where?

EDMOND
Anywhere. I have a ship anchored in the harbor. We can sail immediately. All of us.

(ALBERT and MERCEDES share a look)

ALBERT
Count, that is an invitation we cannot accept.

EDMOND
I see. May I ask why?

ALBERT
I did not put aside the title of Morcerf because it shamed me. I put it aside because I was no longer worthy of it. I go now to search for the honor that was lost. And you? What do you search for now?

EDMOND
I don't know.

ALBERT
You? The Count of Monte Cristo, who used the world as his chess board, and saw every move before it was played? But now the game is ended. You've won. Now what? *(Pause)* Farewell, Count. I hope we meet again. *(ALBERT picks up his bag)*

MERCEDES
I'll walk with you to the quay.

EDMOND
Mercedes—

MERCEDES
Goodbye, Edmond.

(ALBERT and MERCEDES exit. HAYDEE enters)

EDMOND
Haydee. You know you are free now. You must assume your proper position in society. You are the daughter of a prince.

HAYDEE
If you say so, my lord.

EDMOND
Is that not what you wanted?

HAYDEE
I thought it was. But now...

EDMOND
Have we deceived ourselves? Did we follow a false path? Can it be that the work upon which we founded all our hopes was an impossible, nay, a sacrilegious, undertaking?

HAYDEE
I don't know, my lord.

EDMOND
It can't be. I would go mad. I am going mad.

(EDMOND collapses. HAYDEE rushes to him)

EDMOND
I don't know what to do. Tell me. Tell me what to do.

HAYDEE
We must wait, and hope.

EDMOND
For what?

(The lights narrow. EDMOND and HAYDEE are left alone in a small island of light)

End of Play

ABOUT THE AUTHOR

Alexandre Dumas, born Dumas Davy de la Pailleterie on July 24, 1802, in Villers-Cotterêts, was a French writer best known for his numerous historical novels of high adventure which have made him one of the most widely read French authors in the world. Many of his novels, including THE COUNT OF MONTE CRISTO, THE THREE MUSKETEERS, THE MAN IN THE IRON MASK, and THE VICOMTE DE BRAGELONNE were serialized. Dumas also wrote plays and magazine articles, and was a prolific correspondent. These novels made Dumas a household name in France and a popular author throughout much of Europe.

With the money he earned from publishing his novels, Dumas purchased land and built the Château de Monte Cristo in Port Marly, Yvelines, France. This home (which is now a museum) was intended to be a sanctuary for the author, and he spent much of his time writing and entertaining there before debt overtook him, forcing him to sell the property. He fled to Belgium in 1851, and later to Russia, to evade creditors. Dumas continued to publish books, including travel books on Russia, during his period of exile.

ABOUT THE PLAYWRIGHT

Christopher M. Walsh is a writer and actor based in Chicago, IL. He is a member of the artistic ensemble at Lifeline Theatre (Chicago, IL), a member of the Dramatists Guild, SAG-AFTRA, and an Equity Membership Candidate.

His original Sherlock Holmes pastiche *Miss Holmes*, developed and first produced at Lifeline Theatre in Chicago, is available through Dramatic Publishing. His adaptations of *The Count of Monte Cristo* by Alexandre Dumas and *A Tale of Two Cities* by Charles Dickens, also originally produced by Lifeline Theatre, are published by Sordelet Ink, and are available for purchase through Amazon and Barnes & Noble. Other plays include an adaptation of the sci-fi/noir detective story *The City & The City* by China Miéville, and a musical adaptation of *Soon I Will Be Invincible* by Austin Grossman, written in collaboration with composer/lyricist Christopher Kriz. He was nominated for a Jeff Award in 2014 for *A Tale of Two Cities*, and his radio play *Fracture Zone* won the coveted Bloody Axe Award in WildClaw Theatre's 2014 Deathscribe: The International Festival of Horror Radio Plays.

Originally from Muskegon, MI, he moved to Chicago to study acting at Columbia College. He makes his home on the city's North Side with his wife Mandy.

ABOUT LIFELINE THEATRE

Lifeline Theatre is driven by a passion for story. The ensemble process supports writers in the development of literary adaptations and new work, while their theatrical and educational programs foster a lifelong engagement with literature and the arts. A cultural anchor of the Rogers Park neighborhood in Chicago, they are committed to deepening their connection to an ever-growing family of artists and audiences, both near and far.

Lifeline Theatre's history of extraordinary world premiere adaptations includes MainStage productions of PRIDE & PREJUDICE, THE OVERCOAT, THE LEFT HAND OF DARKNESS, THE TALISMAN RING, JANE EYRE, CAT'S CRADLE, AROUND THE WORLD IN 80 DAYS, THE KILLER ANGELS, A ROOM WITH A VIEW, THE ISLAND OF DR. MOREAU, THE MARK OF ZORRO, MARIETTE IN ECSTASY, NEVERWHERE, THE MOONSTONE, WATERSHIP DOWN, and THE COUNT OF MONTE CRISTO.

Lifeline also produced world premiere adaptations of J. R. R. Tolkein's THE LORD OF THE RINGS trilogy (THE FELLOWSHIP OF THE RING, THE TWO TOWERS, AND THE RETURN OF THE RING) and four installments of the Dorothy L. Sayers Lord Peter Wimsey mysteries (WHOSE BODY?, STRONG POISON, GAUDY NIGHT, and BUSMAN'S HONEYMOON).

Family MainStage productions have included A WRINKLE IN TIME, LIZARD MUSIC, THE SNARKOUT BOYS AND THE AVACADO OF DEATH, THE PHANTOM TOLLBOOTH, JOURNEY OF THE SPARROWS, THE SILVER CHAIR, JOHNNY TREMAIN, and TREASURE ISLAND.

In 1986 Lifeline inaugurated its KidSeries program. Productions have included MR. POPPER'S PENGUINS, MIKE MULLIGAN AND HIS STEAM SHOVEL, BUNNICULA, JAMES AND THE GIANT PEACH, THE STORY OF FERDINAND, MRS. PIGGLE-WIGGLE, MY FATHER'S DRAGON, CLICK CLACK MOO: COWS THAT TYPE, THE STINKY CHEESE MAN, DUCK FOR PRESIDENT, THE TRUE STORY OF THE 3 LITTLE PIGS!, THE VELVETEEN RABBIT, THE LAST OF THE DRAGONS, and ARNIE THE DOUGHNUT.

Plays commissioned by Lifeline Theatre have gone on to publication, numerous regional and national tours, and to more than a hundred subsequent productions across over forty U.S. states, five Canadian provinces, as well as in England and Ireland.

FOR MORE INFORMATION
VISIT WWW.LIFELINETHEATRE.COM

MORE FROM SORDELET INK
PLAYSCRIPTS

ACTION MOVIE – THE PLAY BY JOE FOUST AND RICHARD RAGSDALE
ALL CHILDISH THINGS BY JOSEPH ZETTELMAIER
CAPTAIN BLOOD ADAPTED BY DAVID RICE
THE COUNT OF MONTE CRISTO ADAPTED BY CHRISTOPHER M WALSH
DEAD MAN'S SHOES BY JOSEPH ZETTELMAIER
THE DECADE DANCE BY JOSEPH ZETTELMAIER
EBENEZER: A CHRISTMAS PLAY BY JOSEPH ZETTELMAIER
EVE OF IDES – A PLAY BY DAVID BLIXT
FRANKENSTEIN ADAPTED BY ROBERT KAUZLARIC
THE GRAVEDIGGER: A FRANKENSTEIN PLAY BY JOSEPH ZETTELMAIER
HATFIELD & McCOY BY SHAWN PFAUTSCH
HER MAJESTY'S WILL ADAPTED BY ROBERT KAUZLARIC
IT CAME FROM MARS BY JOSEPH ZETTELMAIER
THE LEAGUE OF AWESOME BY CORRBETTE PASKO AND SARA SEVIGNY
THE MOONSTONE ADAPTED BY ROBERT KAUZLARIC
NORTHERN AGGRESSION BY JOSEPH ZETTELMAIER
ONCE A PONZI TIME BY JOE FOUST
THE RENAISSANCE MAN BY JOSEPH ZETTELMAIER
THE SCULLERY MAID BY JOSEPH ZETTELMAIER
ANTON CHEKHOV'S THE SEAGULL ADAPTED BY JANICE L BLIXT
SEASON ON THE LINE BY SHAWN PFAUTSCH
STAGE FRIGHT: A HORROR ANTHOLOGY BY JOSEPH ZETTELMAIER
A TALE OF TWO CITIES ADAPTED BY CHRISTOPHER M WALSH
WILLIAMSTON ANTHOLOGY: VOLUME 1
WILLIAMSTON ANTHOLOGY: VOLUME 2

WWW.SORDELETINK.COM

Sordelet Ink Novels by David Blixt

Nellie Bly
What Girls Are Good For
Charity Girl
Clever Girl

The Star-Cross'd Series
The Master Of Verona
Voice Of The Falconer
Fortune's Fool
The Prince's Doom
Varnish'd Faces: Star-Cross'd Short Stories

Will & Kit
Her Majesty's Will

The Colossus Series
Colossus: Stone & Steel
Colossus: The Four Emperors

Eve of Ides – a play

non-fiction
Shakespeare's Secrets: Romeo & Juliet
Tomorrow, and Tomorrow: Essays on Macbeth
Fighting Words

THE MYSTERY OF CENTRAL PARK

A rejected marriage proposal and the corpse of a dead beauty confound Dick Treadwell's hopes for happiness, until his beloved Penelope sets him a task: she will marry him if he solves—
the Mystery of Central Park!

EVA, THE ADVENTURESS

Nellie Bly's ripped-from-the-headlines novel of a poor girl determined to revenge herself upon the world, only to find that, in the battle between love and revenge, only one can triumph.

NEW YORK BY NIGHT

Setting out to solve the bold diamond robbery, millionaire detective Lionel Dangerfield finds himself in competition with Ruby Sharpe, daring young reporter for the *New York Planet*. Will "The Danger" solve the case before Ruby can steal the story—and his heart?

ALTA LYNN, M.D.

A prank goes awry and Alta Lynn finds herself wed against her will. Leaving love behind, she throws herself into the study of medicine, only to find that love has other plans for her!

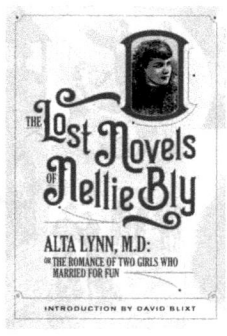

WAYNE'S FAITHFUL SWEETHEART

Beautiful Dorette Lover is rescued from poverty when she finds work as an artist's model. That same day she witnesses a seeming murder. To protect the man accused, she agrees to become his bride—only to fall desperately in love with him!

LITTLE LUCKIE

Luckie Thurlow longs for to be accepted by society and gain the man she loves. But she harbors a dark secret—she is the daughter of the murderous Gypsy Queen, who plans to use Luckie to gain her own revenge!

IN LOVE WITH A STRANGER

Kit Clarendon is in love! Trouble is, she doesn't know her love's name. But she is determined to track him down and force him to love her! A wild pursuit filled with disguises, desperate deeds, and declarations of love as Kit determines to go through fire and water to win him!

THE LOVE OF THREE GIRLS

An heiress in disguise, a factory girl with dreams of wealth, and a sweet child of charity are forced into rivalry when they all fall in love with the same man! Murder, fever, fallen women, and a desperate villain conspire against—
the love of three girls!

LITTLE PENNY

Two young women must flee their troubled homes, forced into lives of hardship and poverty in New York City. Drawn together by fate, they soon become fierce allies in their shared struggle to build a happier future.

PRETTY MERRIBELLE

Trapped in a burning factory, pretty Merribelle's life is saved—but not her memory! A bizarre tale of amnesia, desperate love, and an even more desperate villain determined to use Merribelle to ruin his rival and achieve an inheritance worth millions!

TWINS AND RIVALS

Dimple and Della may be twins, but they have differing views on love. Dimple sees love as a contract, and marries for wealth to support her family, while Della longs to marry for love. The sisters collide when Dimple falls in love with Della's betrothed, turning them into rivals!

THE LOST NOVELS OF NELLIE BLY

ON SALE NOW FROM
SORDELET INK
WWW.SORDELETINK.COM

INTO THE MADHOUSE

Never before collected! "Who is this insane girl?" asked other papers, completely taken in by Nellie Bly's plan to infiltrate Blackwell's Island. The complete reporting surrounding her daring expose, including details not included in her initial accounts and her scathing rebuttal of the doctors' excuses!

NELLIE BLY'S WORLD - Vol. 1
1887-1888

Bly's complete reporting, collected for the very first time! Starting with the stunt that made hers a household name, Nellie Bly spends her first year at the New York World going undercover to expose frauds, sharpsters and boodlers, interviewing Belva Lockwood and Hangman Joe, and tackling Phelps the Lobbyist!

NELLIE BLY'S WORLD - Vol. 2
1889-1890

Bly's complete reporting, collected for the very first time! Nellie buys a baby, has herself followed by a detective and arrested, interviews Helen Keller, champion boxer John Sullivan, and convicted would-be killer Eva Hamilton, all before setting out on her greatest stunt of all, a race around the world!

COMING SOON:

NELLIE BLY'S WORLD, Vol. 3 & 4
NELLIE BLY'S DISPATCHES, Vol. 1 & 2
NELLIE BLY's JOURNALS, Vol. 1 & 2

ALL FROM SORDELET INK

Check Out This Other Great Adaptation By
CHRISTOPHER M. WALSH

ON SALE NOW FROM
SORDELET INK

www.ingramcontent.com/pod-product-compliance
Lightning Source LLC
Chambersburg PA
CBHW061648040426
42446CB00010B/1642